CULTIVATING DIAMONDS

IHOR PAVLYUK

People's poet of Ukraine

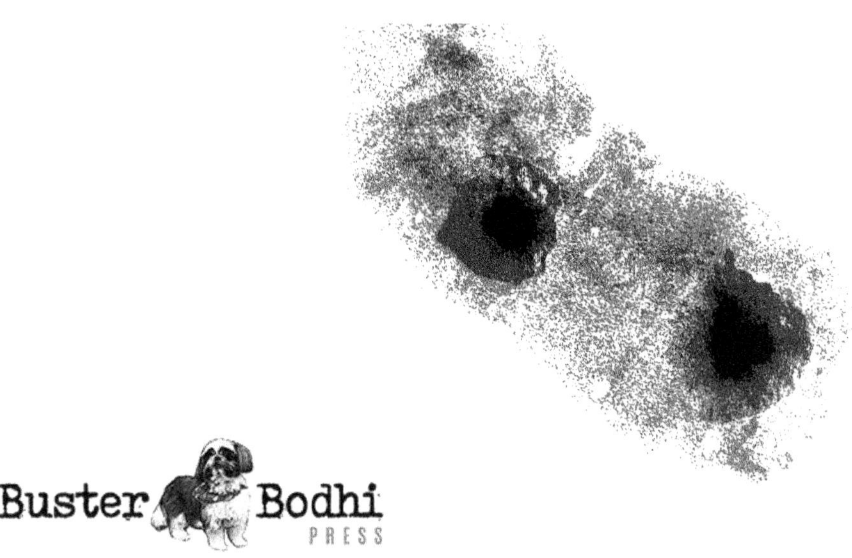

Published by Buster Bodhi Press, LLC

Library of Congress Control Number: 2026934583
ISBN 979-8-9991504-5-5

Edited by Joseph Cavanaugh
Translated from Ukrainian to English by Matvii Smirnov
Cover and book design by Mark Andrew James Terry
Available on Amazon.com, Barnes & Noble online, and most online book sellers

Printed in the USA.

INTRODUCTION

Buster Bodhi Press is proud to publish this first English translation of *Cultivating Diamonds*, a philosophical novel along with a collection of poems by the People's Poet of Ukraine, Ihor Pavlyuk – an internationally-recognized poet, prose writer, playwright, and scholar, whose body of work stands as a testament to the struggle for freedom, dignity, and spiritual endurance universal to the human condition. Poet Naomi Foyle has told us that, "In this time of global isolation and uncertainty, his poetry reminds us that we all belong to this earth – and the cosmos."

Ihor Pavlyuk is a true poet of the people, calling us to remember the strength and beauty that exists in our shared history, and urging us to have hope for the future; to see the dignity and power that is within us. This world needs voices like his. It is our sincere hope that reading these pages you find that you resonate with his love for his country and humanity, and his indomitable strength and courage.

Joseph Cavanaugh,
Partner, Buster Bodhi Press, and
President of National Federation of State Poetry Societies

with

Mark Andrew James Terry,
Partner, Buster Bodhi Press, and
President of Florida State Poets Association

PREFACE TO CULTIVATING DIAMONDS

Cultivating Diamonds is a philosophical novel by Ihor Pavlyuk translated into English by Matvii Smirnov. This story invites readers to dive deep into the existential diamonds of human beings. This book blurs the lines between reality and philosophy, and the cultivation of one's self becomes as intricate and valuable as the creation of a diamond.

In a world that often prioritizes aridity, haste, clumsy superficiality and rapid gratification, Pavlyuk's narrative inspires us to reflect on what it truly means to be human. It asks us to consider the philosophical implications of our choices, the nature of our connections, and the essence of our experiences.

The title *Cultivating Diamonds* is a powerful metaphor for the human soul, just as nature requires millions of years to create a diamond, this novel suggests that developing one's character and soul takes time, effort, and the right conditions. "Good things come to those who wait," and this sentiment echoes throughout Pavlyuk's story. Each character in his novel represents a different facet of the human experience, grappling with their own struggles and triumphs as they seek to refine their inner diamonds.

The unity of organic versus synthetic cultivation is a recurring theme. While humanity has learned to create artificial diamonds, the novel poses an essential question: who, or what, can cultivate the diamonds of the human soul? This inquiry reflects a deep philosophical concern about authenticity in a world increasingly dominated by artificiality. In a culture that often values surface-level achievements over genuine connections, Pavlyuk's exploration of these themes is both timely and necessary.

Pavlyuk populates his narrative with characters that embody extremes—be it in their emotions, beliefs, or experiences. From soldiers in a war-torn landscape to individuals seeking spiritual enlightenment, each character offers a unique perspective on the philosophical questions at hand.

For instance, Edik Pyzhlietsov and Kostia Kivertsov, two soldiers, engage in banter that reveals their coping mechanisms in the face of chaos. Their interactions are laced with humor, yet they also reflect a deeper existential struggle. As they navigate their harsh realities, they embody the idea that laughter can be a form of resistance, a way to find light in the darkest of times. This resonates with the spirit of resilience, where humor often serves as a coping strategy in the face of adversity.

Moreover, the character of Loa serves as a philosophical guide, providing insights into the nature of existence and the human experience. His reflections in the "Diary" challenge readers to consider the moral implications of their actions and the interconnectedness of all beings. This aligns with the ethos of individualism tempered by a sense of community responsibility, prompting readers to reflect on their roles within the larger tapestry of life.

At its core, *Cultivating Diamonds* is a philosophical dialogue about the essence of life. This novel grapples with fundamental questions: What does it mean to live authentically? How do we cultivate our inner selves amidst the noise of contemporary metamodern life? Pavlyuk's characters often find themselves at a crossroads, faced with decisions that will shape their destinies.

This exploration of authenticity is particularly relevant to today's society, where social media and instant gratification can lead to a superficial understanding of self-worth. The characters' journeys remind us that true fulfillment comes not from external validation but from an inner journey of self-discovery. "You do you," and this novel encourages readers to embrace their unique paths, however challenging they may be.

The philosophical inquiries presented in this novel also engage with themes of love, pain, and the human condition. The characters' experiences reflect the idea that pain is an integral part of the human experience, a necessary component for growth and transformation. Well, "no pain, no gain," emphasizing the importance of struggle in the cultivation of our inner diamonds.

Pavlyuk's novel also outlines the relationship between nature and nurture in shaping human character. The lush descriptions of the natural world serve as a backdrop for the characters' internal struggles, illustrating the profound impact of the environment on personal development. This theme resonates with the belief in the power of the individual to overcome circumstances, echoing the notion that while we may be shaped by our surroundings, we also have the agency to forge our own paths.

The novel's central theme – "How strong you must be to allow yourself to be weak!" – serves as a poignant reminder that true strength lies not in the absence of weakness, but in the courage to embrace it.

Pavlyuk's narrative unfolds against a backdrop of existential inquiry, where characters navigate their desires, fears, and the often-painful realities of life. The interplay between space and time, love and loss, and the pursuit of artistic authenticity resonates throughout the text, urging readers to reflect on their own lives and the societal constructs that shape their experiences. This preface aims to elucidate the key philosophical issues present in the novel and offering insights for the American reader into the rich tapestry of Pavlyuk's storytelling.

At the heart of Pavlyuk's narrative lies the exploration of strength and vulnerability. In a society that often equates strength with stoicism and emotional detachment, Pavlyuk invites readers to reconsider what it means to be truly strong. The characters in the novel exemplify this struggle, as they confront their own weaknesses and the societal expectations that dictate their behavior.

This theme resonates with the philosophical ideas of thinkers like Friedrich Nietzsche, who posited that true strength arises from the acceptance of one's vulnerabilities. The characters' journeys reflect a quest for authenticity, as they grapple with their desires and the fear of rejection. In this context, vulnerability becomes a source of power, enabling individuals to forge deeper connections with themselves and others.

Pavlyuk's exploration of love transcends mere romantic affection; it portrays the spiritual dimensions of human being. The characters' experiences of love are portrayed as transformative forces that challenge their perceptions of self and the world around them. This notion aligns with the idea that love is not only an emotional experience but also a spiritual one—a theme echoed in many philosophical traditions.

A significant philosophical issue in Pavlyuk's novel is the quest for authenticity in arts. The dialogue between characters regarding the nature of true art raises questions about the value of traditional versus avant-garde forms of expression. This discourse reflects a broader cultural conversation about the role of the artist in society and the expectations placed upon them..

The characters in Pavlyuk's novel are shaped by their circumstances, revealing the relationship between external factors and personal creativity. The narrative emphasizes that while an artist's environment can influence their work, it is ultimately the internal struggles and resilience that define their artistic journey. This theme resonates with the philosophical notion that creativity emerges from the interplay of individual agency and societal constraints.

The exploration of strength, vulnerability, love, and authenticity transcends cultural boundaries, offering valuable insights into the human experience. In a society that often prioritizes individualism and success, Pavlyuk's emphasis on the importance of connection and emotional depth serves as a poignant reminder of our shared humanity.

Moreover, the novel's exploration of artistic authenticity challenges readers to consider their own perceptions of art and creativity. In an era marked by rapid technological advancements and shifting cultural norms, the questions raised by Pavlyuk regarding the nature of true artistry remain relevant. The dialogue between traditional and avant-garde forms of expression encourages American readers to reflect on their own artistic preferences and the societal expectations that inform them.

Pavlyuk's novel stands as a testament to the complexities of the human experience, inviting readers to engage with its philosophical themes and reflect on their own lives. The exploration of strength and vulnerability, love and spirituality, and the quest for authenticity in art resonates deeply in a world often characterized by superficiality and distraction. As we navigate the intricacies of existence, Pavlyuk's narrative urges us to embrace our vulnerabilities, seek genuine connections, and pursue our creative passions with courage and authenticity.

Finally, *Cultivating Diamonds* is a quest for meaning—a journey that transcends cultural boundaries and speaks to the universal human experience.

In a society often characterized by a fast-paced lifestyle and a focus on material success, Pavlyuk's narrative is a reminder of the importance of introspection and self-awareness. It challenges readers to slow down, reflect, and consider what truly matters in their lives. The characters' struggles and triumphs remind us that the journey toward self-realization is not only valid but essential.

As you embark on this journey through *Cultivating Diamonds*, I invite you to embrace the complexity of existence. Allow the characters' experiences to resonate with your own and engage with the philosophical questions that arise. This novel is an invitation to reflect on your own life, your relationships, and the cultivation of your inner self.

In the words of Ralph Waldo Emerson, "The only person you are destined to become is the person you decide to be." Let this novel inspire you to cultivate your own diamond, embracing the strength found in vulnerability and the beauty of the human experience. Welcome to the world of Ihor Pavlyuk—a world where every diamond has a story, and every story is a step toward understanding the essence of life itself. This novel suggests that cultivating our inner diamonds requires not only introspection but also a deep connection to the world around us.

Dmytro Drozdovskyi,
Managing editor-in-chief of the Ukrainian magazine of translations "Vsesvit" ("Всесвіт"), PhD, Academic Fellow of the Shevchenko Institute of Literature of the National Academy of Sciences of Ukraine, Kyiv, Ukraine

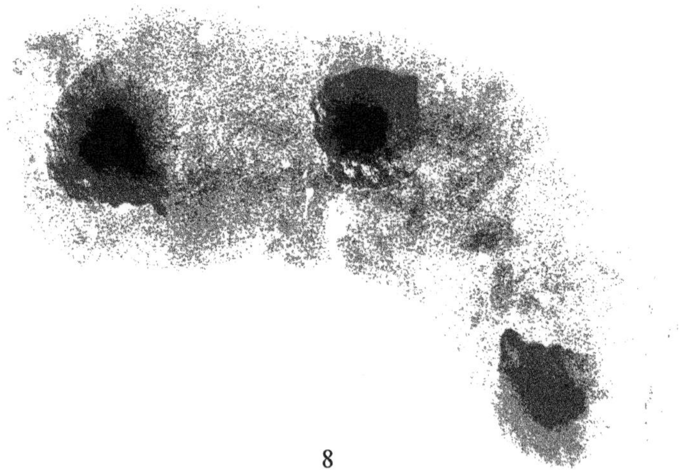

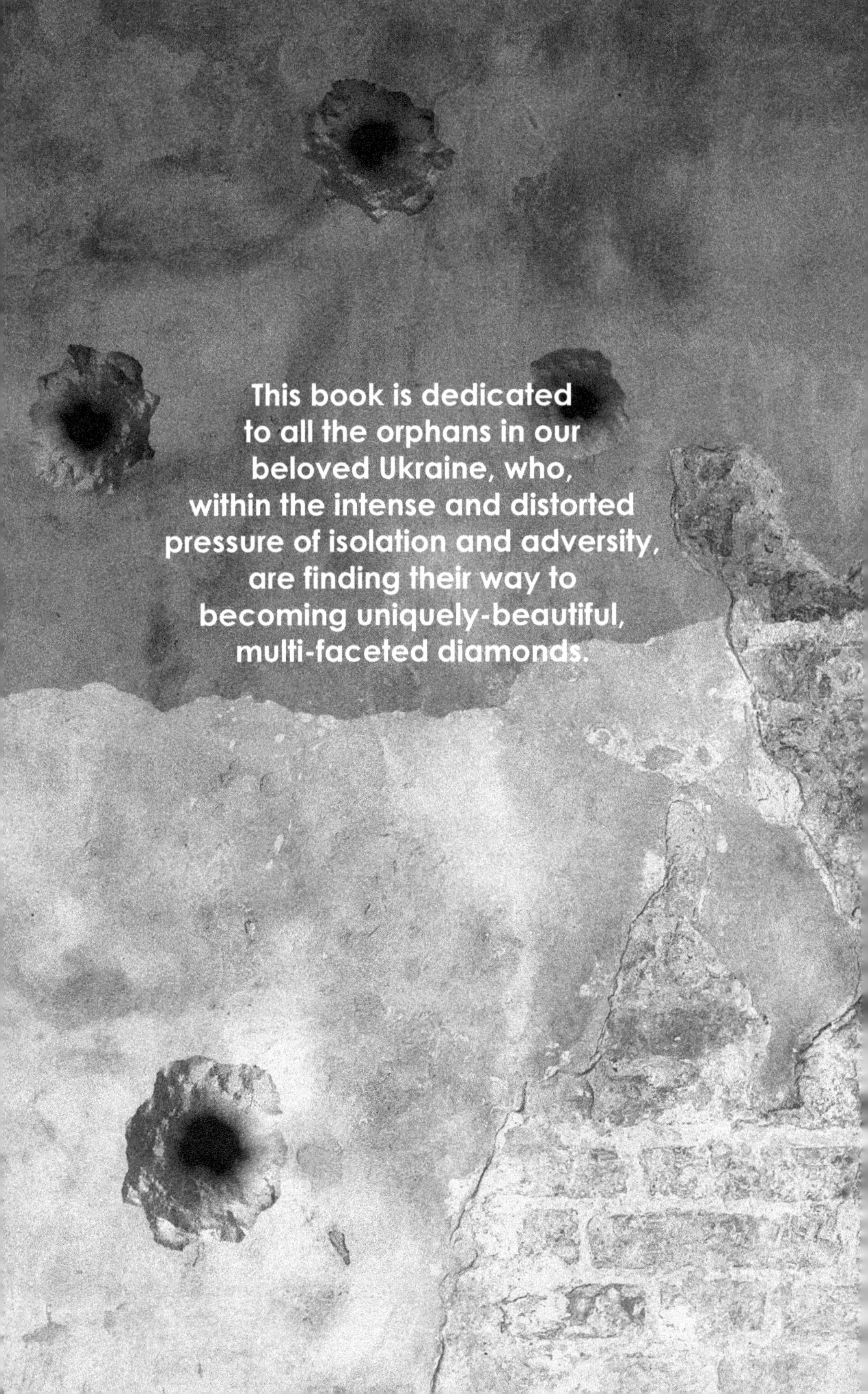

This book is dedicated
to all the orphans in our
beloved Ukraine, who,
within the intense and distorted
pressure of isolation and adversity,
are finding their way to
becoming uniquely-beautiful,
multi-faceted diamonds.

**EDITORIAL OVERSIGHT
OF TRANSLATION:
MATVII SMIRNOV**

Nature takes millions of years to create a diamond. Humanity has learned to grow them artificially...But who, what, and how grows and polishes the diamonds of human souls?... Philosophical, psychological, and ideological questions – between the organic and the synthetic, honor and advantage, outer and inner cosmos – preoccupy the extreme characters of Ihor Pavlyuk's philosophical-science fiction novel – and the author himself.

—Zu fragmentarisch ist Welt und Leben
(Too fragmentary are the world and life)
H. Heine

I

CONVOY

THE SCIENCE OF WAR

Men were cleaning their guns.

Edik Pyzhlietsov was peeing at an anthill.

The suffocating spruce forest, cosy and homely, smiled at the early autumn evening star until it broke loose and fell between the roots.

"Didn't make it," see Kostia Kivertsov said excitedly. "Ah, look over there, see that big one!" He pointed a finger at the sky.

"Ah, fuck it," Edik snorted. "Better spark me up." And he reached with his sticky, sausage-like fingers toward Kostia's lips.

Kostia Kivertsov didn't smoke regularly, but some cheap cigarettes were always lying around in the pockets of his generous uniform trousers. Strangely clean and crumpled, those cigarettes were long and kind of urban-looking, just like Kostia himself, a native of Leningrad.

"Hey, you lip-smacker, what, can't you hear?..."

Pyzhlietsov was born in Odessa...

"Private Pyzhlietsov!" thundered the "Boss", Sergeant Mukharov.

"Coming..."

His "stompers," worn down between the legs, stirred the smell of rotten leaves. A breath of emptiness wafted in the evening October Universe, with a hint of the rough smell of tarpaulin.

"You really made a mess," said Mukharov, who resembled a gibbon, an Oryol native who was six years older than the cadets of the platoon, last year's high school graduates. He had finished a construction college and joined the military school straight after army service. He stood solidly, like a bag of concrete, seemingly with every edge of his body, having written in his notebook: *"Man is a wolf to man."* That notebook would always lie open everywhere. At the same time, it was never heard that he had ever lost it… that it had disappeared, been stolen…

Mukharov was a wolf who claimed to be the leader of a pack that was not a pack of wolves.

"Pyzhlietsov, what are you doing over there?"

"Pissing, comrade sergeant." "And who the hell gave you permission, you motherfucker...?" "Well..." "Mother...land," said Kivertsov, as usual, sparing with words.

Edik, you always have some grub lying around in your bag. Got any biscuits?.." Mukharov, childishly impudent, dug into Pyzhlietsov's thick and slimy bag – and pulled out a mouldy doughnut..."Anything else?.. Oh, wafers!"

A whole pack of recently bought "chow" was eagerly exposed and disappeared into the greedy hole. Its paper wrapper fell casually onto the anthill. Along with it – crumbs of its sweet body, hairs, eyelashes...The ants sensed the sweetness...

"They like piss and wafers alike..." Pyzhlietsov grimaced, prodding the insect society with his boot, and swallowed his saliva that grew sweet.

"Brazen..." Mukharov uttered. He knew people well, in his own way, that was the only thing he knew. He seemed strong at it. Everything else – organic and inorganic nature – was just a means to survive. Wolves were the same. They were just lazier, because their genes had long ago sorted out the problems of eternity, finitude, death. Mukharov, however, needed those same wafers to fuel his brain – to think about death, or to somehow rewire and reprogram his body to get rid of this appendix of consciousness once and for all. To savour power-life and...who the hell knows. And drifting with the current, you could break dams, if the current was a waterfall and you were at least an oak log. But it was him who, paradoxically, saw only people.

"This, by the way, is formally, purely a Christian principle," Loa wrote in his "Diary." *"Strange..."*

"Who knows what's better...Not loving nature doesn't mean hating it," murmured the old Spruce and sank its thoughts into the root, near which the Mushroom grew. The Spruce's thought awakened the self-satisfied world of the bolete.

"To avoid pain, that's what matters. So what if someone hates me! Well, they'll cut me down, they'll eat me. This Game will just end faster!" he shouted, "it will end for all its participants."

"Pain is stupid, stupid, stupid..." rattled the woodpecker on the spruce. "With self-hypnosis, you can make yourself love it..."

"Now, that's masochism," Kostia Kivertsov said, pointing to Pyzhlietsov's "stomper" covered in ants. "They do bite, you know. They will give some good *Pyzhlietsoving*, you'll see!.."

"You know, Pussycat, there are scientific theories, or hypotheses or whatever, that if these little fuckers were as big as cats, they would become...or maybe they will become, the masters of the world..."

"Uh-huh...they, who, by the way, don't even have a brain, can carry objects many, many dozens of times heavier than themselves."

"Such a 'feral' would grab you by the balls, throw you over its ears – and drag you along as building material or a toy for its little bastard offspring. Can you imagine what sons of a bitch they are!" Edik muttered, shaking his ant-covered leg.

"Look, see, there's another star," Kostia said, trying to distract "the comrade." He didn't know much about nature, rarely paid attention to it, though his attention was very sharp. Kostia had an exceptional memory, was always and everywhere an excellent student, outwardly lazy, slow-moving, calm and unobtrusively omniscient, at least in matters of physics and mathematics. Heavy and unsporty, he was, nevertheless, a secret island of hope for souls that felt prickly and windy or childishly defenseless in this Existence. What else, what else distinguished him?.. Oh, yes. He wasn't an actor – by 90...maybe more percent.

"People are divided into actors, less of actors, and not actors at all," Loa wrote in his diary. Then added, *"and those who know how to pull masks off others...some don't."*

"Nonsense, all of it!" the Sun objected. "There is only one division – into the physical and the spiritual. All other divisions are relevant only within the limits of a specific system. People are all the same, by and large..."

"You know, if you look at a big city from a plane that's landing, it looks very much like this anthill. Everyone's scurrying about. Each one knows what he is doing, endless into the past and future, conscious of where he's heading. But from the sky, it all seems like complete chaos. Just like an anthill," said Boris Voytsitsky as he approached. He, too, lived near the "window to Europe," was a smart, calm "street kid" whose grandfather was a forester and beekeeper somewhere in a distant Belarusian forest. "Night, stars, flowers, honey drips from white bread onto the chest of your Fate, and you want to lick it, lick it up, and you keep getting ready, you keep getting ready...And this aching preparation for the process is remembered longer than the process itself," those were his words. "Happiness is a touch. And beyond that – pain..."

"The memory of touch...the memory of a blow..." Loa wrote in his "Diary."

Voytsitsky was clean, shapely-thin, in some girlish way not repulsive physically...No, no, he didn't have even a hint of a dead point, upon reaching which any system sharply changes poles – like a pendulum of a clock with a dead shrill cuckoo.

He had neither the slightest trace of homosexuality nor any other inclinations deemed sinful by the laws of orthodox religions worldwide. Slightly romantic, Leningrader Boris was close to nature. He loved both his city and his grandfather's apiary. Two masters served him, perhaps...

LOA'S DIARY

Rule: "Whoever among people loves nature has in his soul a sense of the Homeland, the land where the wind of his soul is buried."

"Why do you keep that 'Diary'?" Grass asked Loa.

"Ah, these are drafts for another Programme. Maybe I'll come up with something more interesting. I've grown too old in this body."

Grass kept silent because something was happening next to one of its blades.

Pyzhlietsov pulled a bottle of cologne out of his bag, which he carried around for God knows what reason. As the son of a military man, Edik Galileievich could, for instance, polish his boot with a pat of butter or score a goal into the soul of a sentimental simpleton with a piece of bread.

He pulled out the bottle of cologne, lifted a stone covered in gray pine needles, and smashed the expensive cologne over the anthill. As he did so, he squatted a little, spreading his legs feebly, like an old man.

"What the hell are you doing?!" Voytsitsky shouted, rushing toward him.

But Edik's beautiful silver lighter, which he would also carry around tucked away in his boot, quickly revealed what it was capable of. A blue flame flashed, and the black wax of the swampy-warm evening burned the artificial indifference of the hardened barrels of assault rifles.

The anthill caught fire.

LOA RESEARCH CENTER

"Look at that, look at that!" shouted Time, flustered. "I never thought it could happen so quickly."

"You don't know how to play this computer game, my dear colleague," Space replied.

"Old Loa comes up with such weird programmes these days!"

"Well, why don't you become a programmer yourself, then you'll see if you can do any better...Besides, our computers aren't the latest models."

"There are much better ones out now..."

Space:

"Well, we did just get email set up."

Time:

"But that probably cost a fortune. Nowadays, even the Academy of Sciences isn't exactly rich."

"We have to at least try to catch up with other countries if we can't set the tone ourselves."

"But look, look at the monitor! What are they doing..."

The computer screen was veiled in smoke. Through the smoke, Pyzhlietsov's blood, sprayed out with his breath, splashed across it: Voytsitsky had punched him in the nose. The blood quickly clotted and slid down the glass, like torn mercury.

"What the fuck, you bastard?" Edik screamed, swinging his

rifle at Boris. Voytsitsky, in a rage, struck him again. A cracked tooth crunched and was spat out with saliva, snot, and a bloody broth – straight onto the anthill bonfire.

"Guys, guys! It's the end!" An ant trumpeted to a group of fellow drinkers in a tavern. "Nuclear war! The whole antkind is dead! The end of the world!"

"Apocalypse! Apocalypse!.. The prophets wrote about this long ago!" shrieked an old lady ant, clutching her antennae, while her swarm of grandchildren, already silent, huddled around her...

"Oh God, oh God! Oh God!" echoed from all directions.

The ant world was disappearing, like a glance. The consciousness of its brightest representatives burned faster than their bodies: "The end! It's over! Who is it? What is it?"

Sergeant Mukharov stood up:

"Cadets Voytsitsky and Pyzhlietsov! Two extra duties each!"

"Heh-heh," sneered Repyakhin from Königsberg, skinny, dryly spiteful and hard-working, with Aryan blood in his ears and green pupils.

The cadets surrounded the scene, waiting for a spectacle to go with their bread, but the words of the Boss cooled them off.

LOA'S DIARY

In closed systems, all natural-animal urges of people reek of a cadaverous smell. The army in peacetime is one of the most closed spaces. It's worse than prison because in prison a person has the unwritten right to take pride in their sins, their dark deeds, while boys come to the military school to become happy in the future, and therefore, if not good, then at least communicative...Healthy happiness implies freedom, and freedom implies openness.

"Alright, boys, what's done is done," said "Pussycat" Kivertsov and patted Pyzhlietsov and Voytsitsky on the shoulders. "You know, I once saw this English nature documentary. They filmed the whole ant kingdom. Turns out, ants can't see large objects even a meter away, or something like that. Practically, they don't need to."

"Wait, does that mean they didn't even see Pyzhlietsov?!" cried Musakhardinov, the coal-eyed, wiry, and resilient Russian Tatar.

"Seems like it!" came up Hilburdt, bright, kind and voluminous like a butterfly larva.

Everyone froze into themselves, as if the fight hadn't happened at all. Pyzhlietsov was absentmindedly touching the lower part of his face, and Voytsitsky was licking his fist.

LOA'S DIARY

People have already figured out so much. So what should I do with them? Perhaps destroy them all?.. It would be a shame… Start everything over again? But I am too tired already of these creative torments. I've grown old.

LOA RESEARCH CENTER

The old, intricately inlaid but long-unlubricated doors creaked open. Into the Computer Center stepped a couple, Chance and Fate. Fate carried a bouquet of autumn wildflowers, wearing a knitted, dazzlingly white coat with and an impossibly long red scarf. Chance was fair-haired, his faith looking fresh and youthful.

"So, boys, playing a game?" Chance called out to Time and Space. "Who's in the lead?"

"For now, it's Space," Time replied.

"Loa put together quite the clever program!" Time glanced at the clock and reached for a cup of coffee, which had cooled – forgotten in his excitement over the game – but still buzzed, alive with its lingering energy. "People behave so strangely in here."

"And what's the goal of your task – to wipe them out faster or keep them alive as long as possible?" asked Fate, the iron lady.

"Well, this is how it works – one player plays with their souls in the Cosmos, the other in the Core," Space explained. "Meaning: one side wants to push humanity beyond Earth and settle them across the universe, while the other wants to keep them in the cradle, so to speak."

And Time added:

"Loa, of course, wants to keep them alive for as long as possible..."

"Listen!" his colleague gasped, pressing a long, beam-like and sea-wavy ring to his transparent lips. "Why would you –"

"Isn't it obvious they're on our side? The whole universe has known for ages that Loa's wife is dead."

"But still…"

"It's fine, it's fine, don't be scared or embarrassed," Fate said with playful determination, showing Time both her and Chance's identification cards. "We're here precisely so you can initiate us into Loa's final secret."

"For everyone who needs that, there's email," Space stated firmly.

"But we're not just going to sit around like you, glued to computers. You're programmers. This is your energy."

"So, just stop with the bureaucracy!" Fate trilled sweetly, beautiful yet sharp.

"I mean… who could object to someone like her?" Time winked at Space and handed him some official slip, the emblem of the Sun at its centre. Space passed it to Fate, lingering just slightly as his fingers brushed against hers, charged with magic. Sensing the permission, he playfully wrapped an arm around her slender waist. Fate resisted just enough to keep things interesting, then blew a teasing "Kiss-Kiss Bye-Bye" – and shoved Chance forward like a household servant.

Space snapped his fingers in farewell. The doors closed with a gust of wind. The fragrant, wildflower aura of Fate remained in Loa's Centre, like eternity in infinity.

"What do we have on the screen, huh?" Time cut in.

"Look at them! Look at what these bastards are thinking about!" His colleague grew animated. "Some of them, thanks to intuition, feel their unity with everything – from the star systems down to the atoms – on a genetic level. They're using inductive reasoning. They map the structure of an anthill onto human society – and suddenly realise… that they understand nothing at all! That's power!"

"What if we introduce a few artificial variables?" Time grinned, eagerly grabbing the computer controls. "Say… drop a World War II mine in front of one of these cadets?"

"And who would that be?"

"Storozhuk, the one coming back now…"

MILITARY SCHOOL

A sluggish, yet cunning like an old woman, cadet shuffled toward the platoon. He was from Kryvyi Rih, a city-dweller through and through, yet he looked like a badger that had somehow overdeveloped the upper half of its body. And despite all that, his personality wasn't entirely lost – there was something promising about him. At the very least, he could stand up for himself when needed, even though he was a suck-up. Maybe, just maybe, he could even stand up for someone else?

"Lads!" He threw his arms open wide –

– and then BOOM! – an explosion beneath him, like a landmine.

For an eternal second, only a patch of fresh, startled pine needles remained where Storozhuk had been.

LOA'S DIARY

A horrific situation – yet horrifically banal.

Now everyone will freeze, imagining themselves in the place of the one who was just torn apart. For a fleeting moment, they will feel closer, even united.

Too bad humanity as a whole can't be brought together with the same kind of force. Imagine the raw, living energy that would radiate from that! The founders of the world's religions – Christ, Buddha, Muhammad – have done a lot toward that goal, at least in the strategic sense. But how great would it be to create a single, syncretic religion for all of humanity? It would generate a certain kind of energy, sure – although a dull, diluted kind – sometimes even a true opiate…The great "godless" poets – Byron, Shevchenko, Dante – may produce less energy, but it's undeniably of higher quality: paradoxical, masochistic, exalted. Christ – more than any of them.

At the moment of a religion's birth… In short, I have come to understand: A divine individual generates energy millions of times purer than a crowd worshiping that individual.

I don't want new paths, new religions – all of them, in their own way, are good.

I want more divine individuals.

…Another paradox.

Only paradoxes generate energy.

And that – is the secret…

MILITARY SCHOOL

The trees, bushes, and grasses felt pain too after the explosion. The yellow blood of celandine dripped onto a young plantain. A little dandelion shook off its seeds, but on Storozhuk's blood – perhaps, perhaps they would grow even stronger.

Somewhere far above, a star fell. Then another. And another…

In the hollow of an old, fragrant spruce, squirrels nestled – warm, cosy and fluffy, like the spruce itself. The hollow was lazy, safe, a stark contrast to reality – especially in winter, when the earth's silence was slashed apart by howling blizzards, by snowstorms cold and sharp, like the bloodied glass of dawn.

When the Creator's soul felt heavy, He longed to be that squirrel in the hollow.

"Oh no! Better a marten, better a marten..." murmured the squirrel, startled by the explosion, not knowing what to do with herself or her young – flee into the unknown or wait for the humans to pass…?

LOA'S DIARY

The squirrel wants to become its own enemy, because a marten has all the squirrel's advantages – but is also a predator. It fears no other animals. Victims want to be their killers. The only predator for a marten is a human. Humans destroy all living things on the planet while multiplying at a dizzying speed. At the start of the 20th century, Earth's population was barely one billion, living for millennia with more or less the same technology – the wheel.

Then – 1945. The atomic bomb exploded.

Then – 1961. Humanity burst into space.

And so it began…

Now, there are 7 billion of them.

A technological leap – mirrored by a leap in population. Just as predicted.

Humanity is a cancer in the body of the planet.

All of these accelerated processes generate colossal energy – war, sport… a biological-soulful energy. Second-rate energy.

First-rate energy is the high spiritual flight of an individual soul.

The former – mere stones.

The latter – a gem. A true diamond.

LOA RESEARCH CENTER

Gray-haired Time approached the rain-streaked, yellow-curtained window. He glanced at his noble signet ring:

"Gold… but the Old Man needs diamonds…"

A violet-coloured email wire, like a spiderweb, glazed over his gaze into the early spring. Time waved it away dismissively…

"Have some coffee," said Space, approaching – aged, slightly balding, fox-mannered. "The rules of our game seem to be getting clear. We need to extract everything possible from the planet – within the shortest time frame."

"It's such a fragile thread everything hangs on… On one hand, we must bring Earth to self-destruction. On the other, we must preserve it for as long as possible…"

"A paradox."

"Exactly. But genius is a paradox too. A diamond."

Time paced the room, his noble head bowed in thought.

"At last, the Old Man has realized that spiritual individuals are the key. But they can't be cultivated without a 'normal' environment and without abnormal, highly conflicted conditions and environment."

"Our ninth-generation computer has already registered quite a few geniuses," Space smiled, in a way almost feminine.

"Yes, but it's also filled with scum – scum that Loa will

inevitably destroy on Judgment Day, scattering it like chaff."

"And yet, the criteria remain volatile..."

"As long as they were volatile, Judgment Day remained unknown. But now it's clear: those who carry the least spiritual energy and fail to cultivate it in others – less than a thousand megawings – will be destroyed."

"I suggest we repurpose the 'Earth' laboratory to cultivate only pure diamonds – Dante, Shakespeare, Mozart, Byron, Shevchenko..."

"Experience shows, dear friend, that in sterile conditions, only synthetic diamonds are produced. And there's no way around it."

"Aha. Well, back to work..." Space patted Time on the shoulder. "Let's go prepare the data for Judgment. The Old Man is eager to summarise the past – to begin the second order. Maybe we'll tweak the conditions, the rules of the game...the prayers..."

MILITARY SCHOOL

A month had passed.

On the sea-washed sand – people lay sprawled. Some were dusty like sand, others foamy like waves, others light as the sky... Emerging from the sea, moving, groaning, grasping at the Sun, playing cards, tending to their athletic or flabby bodies.

Meanwhile, on a lush green hill, a ten-minute walk away, the ancient church bells tolled – their chime rolling over the old orchard and the graves of long-forgotten servants of the Lord.

At the command of Lieutenant Colonel Zaskorodny, and – by the principle of chain reaction – Sergeant Mukharov, a squad of armed men swiftly and brutally stripped before charging into the water.

A few minutes later, the order rang out:

"Enough! Enough swimming!"

Like maniacs, they splashed their way onto the shore. The ordinary civilians nearby stepped aside, away from them.

The rifles stood in pyramids, each one guarded by two men.

People shifted. The weapons remained. The bells tolled –

beating like hearts, pumping blood.

"Do you go… did you go to church?" Voytsitsky asked one of the soldiers.

"As a kid, with my gran." The soldier replied.

"And do you believe in God?"

"I think…"

"What's there to think about, you moron? Thinking is for retards. Everything's already been thought through without us." The wobbly Pyzhlietsov butted in.

He pulled a cheap compass from his bag and shuffled forward, penguin-like, towards the soldier.

"Want me to give you a tattoo?" he slightly jabbed the compass into the soldier's back.

The soldier flinched, shoved away Edik's damp, sticky hand – sticky even after the sea. He was physically superior to Pyzhlietsov in every way, but no one could ever make him snap, curse, or – least of all – throw a punch. And yet, he was a sponge, absorbing everything interesting in the world, a sort of vampire, a self-sufficient system in his own right.

Something happened to Pyzhlietsov around him. He lost control of himself, consumed by some force that wanted, at any cost, to disrupt the balance of the soldier's soul.

Again and again, like a wave crashing against the shore, Edik lunged forward with his compass, trying to stab him deeper, more painfully, with a dumb, nasty determination.

The soldier smiled mysteriously, dodging, shifting. After a few minutes, it became clear – deep down, he was conducting his own experiment on Pyzhlietsov's soul, testing its limits, subtly, drop by drop, losing patience only slightly – perhaps after a particularly sharp jab?

Nearby lied baroque-spectacled Yablokov – Pyzhlietsov's external friend. Their only true bond seemed to be a mutual love of pastries from the barracks shop. Yablokov was oddly refined, with aristocratic mannerisms. With a delicate, almost effeminate flick of his ring finger, he adjusted his tinted spectacles, their glass veiled in the faintest, dandy-like haze.

And yet – how strangely dusted crystal and egg-white slipperiness coexisted in him.

Yablokov lay back, waiting for the outcome of the psycho-physical experiment, waiting with a crude impatience – for the bet was simple: If the soldier cursed or lashed out with a punch – Pyzhlietsov gets a cake; if he stayed calm, as always – Yablokov would be the one to get it.

The experiment might have dragged on indefinitely, had it not been interrupted by the sudden buzz of an impudent bee – drawn, no doubt, to the sharp, primal scent of Pyzhlietsov's sweat.

He bolted – charging along the beach, although really, his most natural escape would have been into the sea. But the sea – Edik feared on a genetic level.

At that moment, Dukhmatov approached them all.

"Lads," he said, "enough messing with poor Pyzhlietsov. Anyone off-duty tomorrow – come by mine. I'm a Leningrader, after all..."

A few seconds later, the chain-command echoed across the shore:

"Enough! Get dressed!"

A scramble by the sea began…

LOA RESEARCH CENTER

"Listen, maybe we should change the channel?" Space said to Time. "I'm personally getting tired of these cadets. A hopeless subject for theory. A closed system."

"Run one more episode," replied Time, usually reserved. "And how many times must I tell you – there's no such thing as a 'hopeless' or 'promising' subject? What's a plus in one system is a minus in another – and vice versa. Balance must be preserved."

"Balance, you say...I learned that back in school. But what about plant and animal species that are about to extinct? What about them? Who replaces them? What bio-soul mass?"

(A faint signal from one of the Center's computers...)

"Oh, hear that? Someone's broken through the electronic defense barrier with a prayer again. A prayer has been registered. That hardly ever happens any more."

"Put it on the screen, open the file..."

"Oh, this is a prayer from someone already deceased – for the happiness of their still-living child. In such cases, the program mandates assistance. Put this case on file. We'll have to track it later."

"Even more so – look, gene 24-X-315. It's also in the file where we're testing the new programme, the one we've been playing with."

"Oh wow! So, it's in one of these armed men?"

"Precisely..."

"Switch them back on, my friend. Let's finish watching Dukhmatov's gathering."

"Right..."

MILITARY SCHOOL

Dukhmatov's apartment stunned with its creativity. It was large, layered in dim hues, almost medieval – with webs of scars and scars of webs lurking in the corners.

The disorder was so deep, so cultured, that it felt almost cosy – modestly poor yet homely.

Apartments like this must have especially unsettled young men from remote forest villages in their first months in the big city. Everything here was supposed to be different, richer, loftier, heavenly even. These apartments left them feeling like a naked man wrapped in a sheepskin coat – then shoved into an ice hole.

The shock factor was amplified by the fact that Alexey Dukhmatov's father was a professor at Leningrad University, and his mother – a musician from the conservatory. For a village boy, this was something high and unreachable, something that should have been celestially radiant, both spiritually and materially. But, by the law of extremes flipping into their opposites, the soul – like an egg, like a bearing ball – tilts, rolls, adjusts itself strategically, genetically.

The slippery-smoky body of the soul quickly absorbs the orgiastic atmosphere of high-minded poverty and chaos.

"Boys, boys! Everyone here, please, everyone here," chirped Dukhmatov's mother.

"Some light sandwiches with tea. Rest a little, music… Alexey, Alexey, play something classical for your friends."

They all followed her into the small, time-smoked room of the younger Dukhmatov, where a sturdy, well-worn piano stood, rooted into the floor. The walls – aching for renovation – were covered with his drawings.

It would have been appropriate to remark on the undeniable talent of the artist, as is customary in such situations.

But…

The drawings were so abstract, so avant-garde, as they say...

LOA RESEARCH CENTER

A rain-weathered, forever young Fate walked in. Leaning over Time, she said:

"Look at that… look at how the souls of our people flicker and work, especially that one – 24-X-315. His energy is terrifying."

"He desperately wants to truly appreciate everything related to art. But how can one evaluate what doesn't exist? After all, in art, the most important thing… is art itself."

"As an old professor once said," the noble Time interjected, "I don't know whether it's a cow or a cloud, but as a blot – it might just work."

They all laughed, each finishing the laughter in their own way.

"Look, look at the energy radiating from that 24-X-315," Fate's voice rang out. "He and Voytsitsky have stepped a little away from the group."

MILITARY SCHOOL

"How do you like this painting here, the one labelled 'Painted Dust'?" Voytsitsky asked 24-X-315.

"You know, if there were actual dust here, I'd appreciate it. But these are just dots and geometric figures – pure pretension. If a pretentious poet wants to be genuinely appreciated face-to-face, let him first present a traditional, rhymed stanza about love. Only then should he show his experiments with versification. The same goes for a painter – let him first paint a simple tree outside his window, or a portrait of his cat, or you, or me – someone I can see, someone I know. And only after that… You know, there's this joke: when Picasso was robbed, the police started looking for suspects based on his sketches of the crime scene (he was in the half-empty railway car when he was robbed). They ended up bringing in two vacuum cleaners, a washing machine, and a fountain pen."

"So, you're against all avant-garde?"

"I'm against mediocrity. Talent is from God. That's why it's ridiculous to praise an artist for talent – it's like praising a pot for making good soup. A pot can be praised for the effort that went into cooking and preserving the soup. An artist should be praised for their persistence, for something fundamentally human – not for the divine gift. Because, for all we know, it may be a punishment, not a reward."

"Do circumstances influence an artist?"

"The same way fire influences a pot. Fire can't directly affect the soup. The soul needs work, struggle – that's why only artificial souls grow in sterile conditions."

"So: not everyone with a great, tormented soul is an artist, but every artist possesses a great soul."

"Something like that. But in general, these things belong to the realm of deep intuition, something that binds us to the sky, some-thing beyond our grasp – like ants unable to perceive the humans walking past their anthill. It's simply beyond them – end of story..."

"Hey, guys, what's keeping you? Get over here for tea," Dukhmatov called, nodding his head. At that moment, Voytsitsky was struck by something – how had he never noticed before just how exaggeratedly flexible and flamboyant Dukhmatov's mannerisms were?

Dukhmatov sat at the piano, playing some classical piece. It was clear – behind him stood his entire professor's apartment, all of Leningrad, centuries of noble lineage.

But the sky… the sky was not with him.

The best schools and the cultivated home atmosphere had given him so much – had led him right to the edge of a luminous abyss. Step by step, thousands, millions of patient hours, intellect, an aristocratic, subconscious need to refine, to fulfill, to transcend – had brought him here.

But to take that one more step – small in distance, but infinitely different in meaning, the step where everything truly begins – that, he could not do.

To be pushed over the edge of talent's abyss – that was only Loa's doing, long before a person was even born. Hundreds reach the edge of that abyss but only a few take that last step – a step equal in size to all the ones before it, but in meaning – the difference between sky and earth. Only a handful, the Creator's diamonds, make the leap.

Dukhmatov's mother peeked softly through the door and smiled – like a mother.

Dukhmatov finished playing, restrained, as if giving no weight to his performance.

Better to ironize one's own soul than let it be mocked by the shadows of wrinkles on others' faces.

"Well… who else? Anyone?"

LOA RESEARCH CENTER

Fate and Chance met by chance on a warm, blinding autumn afternoon in the city park. They were both thrilled, delighted by the encounter. They began speaking of nothing, yet with a painful tenderness – fearing flight and yearning for it all the same.

They sat down on a bench. To fill the hopeless void of their arcing pauses, Chance pulled out his mini-computer.

"See? Remember when we dropped by the Centre, the computer lab? I still have their file open in my system. Look – 24-X-315 is there, in that little gathering around the piano…"

Fate switched on her own portable computer.

"You know… Here he is. If you want, I can help you make something of him."

"As a friend?.." Chance looked at the hair of his dream, his voice unsteady.

"As whatever you want… I'm not experienced in all this…"

Chance had no time to answer. And there was no need to.

They were already speaking through their souls.

DUKHMATOV'S APARTMENT

A few seconds later, 24-X-315 was holding a guitar.

He hesitated, then began to sing – timidly, to the words of a poem he had written himself.

The face of Dukhmatov's mother appeared once again in the doorway. It was slowly turning moonlit, magical – darkening, glowing…

CHANCE AND FATE

"Look at how this woman is glowing! She was once 1-K-8, meant to become a diamond, but she didn't make it – ordinary family life did its work. But she still knows how to recognize the diamond light in others. That's all that sometimes remains of wasted diamonds," said Chance.

"The saddest impression is often left by someone who, having at least some original talent as a critic and connoisseur of the Master, aspires to be called a Master themselves. A theater critic who steps onto the stage and performs a role poorly loses credibility as a public judge of art," Fate said, pulling out a delicate, flower-patterned handkerchief and brushing something off Chance's cheek – though perhaps there was nothing there at all."

"Look at how the woman behaves," Chance murmured. "She watches 24-X-315 play, she understands everything, but she doesn't openly show admiration..."

"It's one of two things – either she feels that pearls, diamonds, are being scattered before swine, or it's simply another case of Mozart and Salieri."

"That's something only in the Computer Centre, where Time and Space work, is made visible. It is not for us to know." Chance looked at the beloved face and added: "By the way, we never got around to reading that note together – the one Time so charmingly handed you. We had a bit of a falling-out then..."

"Oh, that's true! I completely forgot about it. How wonderful that we met. I'll find it in my handbag right now," Fate whispered – hot and piercingly happy.

DUKHMATOV'S APARTMENT

Meanwhile, 24-X-315 was singing and playing.

His singing and playing, taken separately, were terribly clumsy, childishly awkward, shy – but together, as a whole, they radiated an astonishing light, an energy.

Everyone was silent.

From behind his mother peeked a small, ribboned head – Alexey's younger sister Alyonka, cradling a self-satisfied hamster. Alyonka fidgeted, and the hamster's tiny nose caught on the faded floral folds of her mother's robe. Just then, from the kitchen came the voice of the head of the household:

"What's going on in there?"

His mother turned sharply toward him. The orphaned hamster slipped from Alyonka's hands.

"Oh God!" cried Dukhmatov's father, approaching the doorway with concern. "The hamster, the hamster, Alyonka! I stepped on the hamster!"

Thus is born the holy commotion – which, like a tangled ball of hair, rolls into the abyss, accompanying birth, death, even love. In a sudden, unexpected break, everyone abandoned the unusual music and rushed over.

"I stepped on it. It's already dead," the silver-haired professor mournfully confirmed.

Alyonka approached the still-warm creature, cupped it in her hands, and wordlessly dissolved into the half-shadows of the apartment – deep, old, and silent.

CHANCE AND FATE

"Do you see now? Why did you have to do that?" Fate sobbed. "Why?"

"You see, Fate, I wanted to show you once again how alike we are, how your strategic program depends on my tactical vigilance," Chance replied, a crease flashing between his brows.

"I don't remember… maybe it's all in my program? Listen, do you think Dukhmatov's mother will say anything to 24-X-315 about the impression he made on her?" Fate gave a bitter smile.

"You know well that a person's talent isn't their achievement; it's a gift from Loa. The achievement is in how they conduct themselves, what they do with their talent. A diamond can just as well be flushed down a toilet."

"Genius and villainy?"

"Uh-huh. Although, villainy is always villainy, but genius…"

DUKHMATOV'S APARTMENT

"It happens, it happens," said Alexey's father.

"They reached for music, and in the process, took a pet's life," his mother added, mysteriously.

"Fate, Chance… And that hamster was paid for with actual money!" muttered the uniformed young men.

"Sit down, finish your time – oh! – your tea." Someone said.

"Let's visit the 'Russian Museum', for example." Hilburdt proposed introspectively.

"And bury Alyonka's hamster on the way."

"Ah, for fuck's …" Pyzhlietsov muttered, spitting to himself.

Since their leave was nearing the end, they all scrambled to get dressed and headed out into Leningrad. Alexey's father, a physics professor, joined them. They took along little Alyonka, her sorrowful face carrying an unexpectedly grown-up sadness as she cradled the small lifeless body wrapped in a doll's dress.

"Let me tell you a story, boys," the professor suddenly interrupted the silence, his voice adopting a rhythmic, marching tone. "something both funny and bitter – like life on this tiny ball of ours. Once, an Orthodox man set off from a Catholic village to a neighboring Orthodox village to attend church. It was winter. He trudged for a long time through the blizzard until he stepped on a frozen bird. He picked it up, tucked it under his coat, and soon forgot about it.

He arrived at the church and, as was proper, began bowing. At that moment, the revived bird poked its beak out from under his coat – right into his eye! And the eye… well, it leaked from the socket."

"And the man?" Sergeant Mukharov interrupted.

"And what would any of us have done?" The professor

continued. "The man roared and… twisted the bird's head off. What happened after that, I don't know."

"And the people?" someone asked.

"People are just people. Imagine it for yourselves," the professor said, "in the end, people are all the same, especially in extreme circumstances."

"Uh-huh… try philosophizing over that," Voytsytsky mumbled to himself. "It's beyond our comprehension. Just as an ant-warrior cannot see a human-warrior, so too does a human-warrior fail to see Loa… Who perhaps is a warrior himself? How many creators are there? Maybe they fight among themselves, just like all living things on earth? A carousel set in motion…"

"What are you always thinking about, Voytsytsky?" Yablokov questioned. "You are being like our friend Shablii. Be simpler and people will gravitate towards you."

"All sorts of vermin… Not you, though." Voytsytsky spat into the Neva from the bridge where they were standing. He did this, just as he swore, very rarely.

"Listen, Boris, let's bet on this – you idiot – you're always brooding over things that are obvious to everyone. Even to the Foreman Chump." Pyzhlietsov sneered.

"With you, it would turn into an argument… And truth, as we know, is born in debates, not quarrels." Voytsytsky said, moving closer to Shablii.

The men in uniform wandered through Leningrad's golden mist – people of different ethnicities, childhoods, and upbringings. The professor accompanied them. They visited art and military museums, took photographs, absorbed the city's history.

Dukhmatov's father spoke about how Leningrad stood on human bones, many of them Ukrainian, Cossack bones. The mood was heavy, fatigued with sorrow. Almost everyone lit a cigarette.

To return to the barracks, they had to pass through the Summer Garden. The Ukrainians recalled their own Shevchenko, who had once sketched one of these statues – or perhaps that one over there. Some of them wondered if geniuses had privileges in the afterlife (if there was one at all) over ordinary mortals. What did that real yet relative immortality among the living give to their souls?

Their thoughts, like the words of their debates, were fragmented, leading nowhere. Everything blended into one – the modern concert, the eternally sealed canvases in the Russian Museum. After all, in the end, what matters in art is the proportion of art itself, not the number of variations.

And maybe art isn't even that important at all…

CHANCE AND FATE

"You see, Chance." Fate turned to her companion, sharp yet tender. "Look at the thoughts surfacing in the people we're observing right now. Is art really important? It doesn't save humanity as a whole, but it helps certain sensitive souls survive – thus, in the end, preserving humanity itself. And humanity, in turn, survives by consuming everything else – draining the Earth's oil-blood, paving its skin with asphalt, killing and devouring other species for no reason at all. Have you seen how they panic when, say, a tiger escapes from a zoo and mauls some drunk? The television, radio, newspapers all scream in horror – oh, the tragedy! But what about the countless starving, suffering cats wandering the streets, the basements, the student dormitories? No one cares."

"It's the law of competition, Fate. You know that..." Chance replied, his voice filled with quiet adoration. "And what is left for us, fools, to sit here drinking tea? They, in the Computer Centre, have access to everything, while we are merely pawns following orders. We are Loa's soldiers."

"Loa's soldiers," Fate echoed. "Or angels, as humans call them. In our terms – sensors, bridges, record keepers of the heart-mind of every living being, of flora and fauna, across all the laboratories of the universe. When a creature dies, these sensors are transferred into the disks of the computer, becoming seed material for future genetic experiments."

"Don't you think our lives are just a game, a game without a real goal? Our lives, yours and mine?"

"Yes," Chance admitted, taking Fate's trembling fingers into his own. "But I think they've sensed that at the Centre… That was my impression last time we were there. By the way, have you forgotten about the note that Time so charmingly, so teasingly handed to you?"

"Oh, you're right!" Fate exclaimed with childlike delight, rummaging through her elegant handbag. "Here it is! Sealed."

"Go on, open it."

Pressed close together, Chance and Fate eagerly unfolded the little slip of paper – "entirely oblivious to the passage of time", so to speak. Their imperceptible seconds might have spanned years, even centuries, in the world of humans. After all, animals, as humans liked to believe, did not grieve lost time, did not know about death, and, just as humans liked to think, they knew nothing of love – the very act they engaged in with unthinking pleasure.

The note held a message:

"Yesterday, Loa's wife died. Humans, in their naivety, saw her as his opposite – Satan. To survive, Loa has only one option: to become self-sufficient – both man and woman. For this, he requires immense spiritual and physical energy, above all the energy of genius-diamonds, those rare points around which, as we know, all types of energy accumulate. We are cultivating diamonds. Find the material – act, now."

"...And signed: Space-and-Time," Chance read aloud. "Well, there you have it."

For the first time in his existence, he pulled Fate close, holding her tight, a surge of energy between them. Lightly, like a breath of wind, he kissed her lips.

Fate's red cloak flared like a leaf caught in a scorching blue wind. She was already on her way.

Autumn flowers chimed.

A painful, bittersweet anticipation filled the air.

ANCESTORS

...They cut him down with no poetry. The wind was blowing, so there were no butterflies. Where there is fear, there is no romance...

The gothic churchyard rain streamed down, washing crimson leaves from the maple children. Human blood, thin and fluid, yields just as easily to even the mildest water. But saltwater – tears –

washes bloodstained stones of souls along with their very roots.

What a strange root the soul-stone has!

LOA RESEARCH CENTRE

"What a strange root the soul-stone has!" cried noble Time to Space.

"Look, look – medieval executions of Ukrainian Cossacks in Polish town squares."

"There is something oddly cosy in that medieval spirit, though so brutally cruel," murmured Space.

"From a distance, and especially on a computer screen, anything can seem cosy. Even this..." Time pressed a button on the control panel, and at once, the screen burst into a terrifyingly beautiful chaos of dinosaurs, ichthyosaurs, brontosaurs – a bubbling mass of ancient, monstrous life, tangled in the ever-green wilderness of that, in every sense of the word, inhuman era of Earth.

A fine place to visit – if one had a helicopter. Or, at the very least, a Carlson-style propeller strapped to one's back, armed with a laser, clad in a super-protective suit, stocked with provisions and survival gear. In short, a grand adventure – to hunt, to roll around in the wild, primitive hay of a bygone world.

"But tell me, my friend – would you care to face them one on one, naked and unprotected?"

"Listen, Time, you speak far too often on behalf of Humans. You long to experience life in their skin," Space smirked slyly.

"You know why...But anyway, look – look at another image. Here, there are humans, but no dinosaurs. A new era – the era of Man," Time switched the scene.

"Forgive me, but you won't find a single trace of 24-X-315's genetic line among these early tribes. Here, only brute physical strength matters. What diamonds of the soul could possibly emerge here? Loa himself likely had no idea what he had created yet – he was merely playing."

"But listen! If we choose, we can resurrect these souls in a later time, exactly as they were!" Time proposed.

"You know better than anyone – it would be a waste of energy. In this environment, a diamond could never grow. The world is already overflowing with imitations. Creativity may arise among plants and animals, but among evil men..."

"'Evil' and 'primitive' are entirely different things. I'd bet that even among outlaws and prisoners, one might find diamonds of the purest kind."

"Perhaps. But societal demand is necessary. A poet or musician, in a world of primitive tribes like these," Space gestured to the screen, where firelight flickered in the hands of early humans, "is an unrecognized entity. Though! Look – soon they will have priests, shamans, spell-weavers… Perhaps they are the first diamonds? Let's skip ahead a few centuries."

Time pressed another button.

"Let's set the coordinates for 24-X-315's genetic signature… Space, Space! There! There it is!" Time shouted. "Look, I've found the gene! See – there he is, crouching under a sprawling pine, like a rabbit… walking toward the cliff -side…"

Space lunged toward the screen.

"You see, it's all happening by the sea. The sun shines, the wind stirs, everything is wild and green. Here, you can truly feel the genius of Loa."

24-X-315 approached a cliff by the shore. A boat drifted to the coast, and from it stepped a girl – young, childlike in her beauty. Seeing him, she faltered, braced herself, and turned back toward the boat.

He put down his brush made of wildcat fur and paint mixed with grass and blood, slowly, with quiet pride, walked toward her across the sand.

The paint dripped… dripped… Drying on the rock, She took shape.

"Look, Space, he's an artist – one of the first human painters," said Time, his voice solemn. He adjusted the colours on the screen, adding a touch more sunlight.

24-X-315 reached the girl.

"You know… I couldn't…"

"Hello…" she whispered warily.

"I couldn't keep my promise to myself – to ignore you, to live as
if you didn't exist. I failed."

The girl, carrying within her something just as fragile and immense, couldn't hold back – she broke, like an apple from a branch.

"Oh, how wonderful that I found you! How wonderful!" she
whispered, producing a leaf of wild mint and gently brushing the
shadow from his face.

A tenderness of magic trembled between them.

"The beginning of their drama belonged to them alone.
But its unfolding – its artistic legacy – could have belonged
to the entire world."

"Look at the energy radiating from 24-X-315," said Space.

"That's the energy of Love."

"Yes. Real love. Because it is creative."

"But look at what the fool is doing! This artist!" Time
laughed with indulgent irony. He breathed onto his noble signet
ring, polishing it against his sleeve of strange, otherworldly fabric.
"He's painting on the sand of the golden shore!"

"He's painting his dream beside his dream!" Space cried out.

"Don't be fooled," Time turned to him. "That's exactly what
an artist is. Art is an impractical, childlike energy that only belongs
to the Creator and is untouched by earthly transformations."

24-X-315 traced the aching silhouette of his love in the wet sand
with his finger. Speaking to her, painting her – his heart desperate to
consume her with a soul as vast as the sky and sea. But an invisible
force held him back, compelling him to be tender, restrained, and –
without realizing it – to paint his own soul through images.

"See, see!" the artist whispered to the girl, unknowingly
transforming her into a Muse before all living things.

"Kiss her… kiss her…" the waves whispered.

"Embrace her…" the seagulls chanted.

"Love her, love her!" the jellyfish kept silent.

The artist felt their urging, and his hands burned with
tenderness.

He whispered again, "See, see!" – but then, unable to hold back,
he ran toward the cliff, brush in hand, to paint her there, where
the waves could not wash her away.

The girl stretched out her hands, reaching for him as the tide reached for the shore, but she could not grasp her sweetest torment.

The sun was setting. The girl drifted away – yet she remained, taking shape upon the burning rock.

"What a strange man…" Space murmured, agitated. "Why doesn't he…? They love each other! This is everything!"

"He's an artist. And later, he'll torture himself for it. They are paradoxical creatures, these diamonds. Like sponges, they absorb the energy of every grain of sand around them, yet like lenses, they focus it into a single searing point – and then release it. And in the end, they themselves feel hollow, insatiable, and often… poor. Because that's what they are. They are too sensitive – so they seem harsh. Too fragile – so they appear strong. Extremes turn into their opposites. If I had to name them all – the artists of all times and nations – I would call them just one thing: Paradoxes."

LOA'S DIARY

But the greatest paradox is this: a person who loves humanity unconditionally contributes to its preservation and expansion.

Logically this makes sense. Humanity, with giant strides, is destroying its cradle – the laboratory of Earth; draining its oil-blood; asphalting over its soil-skin; polluting its seas and wiping out all forms of life, while multiplying at a terrifying rate. In 1900, there were one billion people; by 1980 – seven billion. That's some acceleration!

The harshest truth is that, from the perspective of the universe, a figure like Hitler is more beneficial than a self-sacrificing, altruistic nun. After all, Hitler helped eliminate millions of people, effectively extending Earth's lifespan. Wars also claim the lives of potential geniuses – minds that, in the future, might have either invented new means of destruction or new ways of preservation, which, paradoxically, amount to the same thing. In short, paradox and struggle are the engines driving the material world through the spiritual and vice versa.

If humanity destroys itself, a massive burst of energy will be released – brute, momentary energy, lacking in quality. If it survives, spreads beyond Earth, and multiplies across the universe, that energy will be dispersed too thinly. The best course of action is to sustain humanity on Earth for as long as possible. And since the purest, most valuable energy is that of diamonds – the work of spiritual geniuses – perpetual spiritual discomfort must be maintained on the planet. There are many ways to achieve this, one of them being material discomfort.

Thus, I will personally oversee the genes of potential geniuses. Let Chance, Fate, Time, and Space handle the animal and plant worlds, as well as ordinary people. That is how it was, is, and will be.

LOA RESEARCH CENTRE

"Listen, Time!" Space stirred, his gaze accidentally sliding over the instructions. "Will it always be like this? Can we intervene at least a little in the lives of the Creator's favorites – the various geniuses?"

"Old friend, haven't we already caused plenty of trouble in this sector?"

"Well, personally, I've toyed with Fate's favorites from time to time, but even Chance dares to joke with Loa's chosen ones more than I do."

"You have a short memory, my friend. Sure, you didn't exile Ovid, torment Dante, or blind Homer. When Pushkin and Lermontov were shot, you didn't blow on the bullets to steer them away from fatal wounds, making sure they only suffered. But by interfering in the lives of ordinary people, we inevitably create the conditions for diamonds to form – their quality, their perception of the world, which many capture in paintings, poems, novels. The truest records are stored with us, on our disks."

"Yes, geniuses do part of the work for all of us, including Loa." Time mused. "They prepare condensed blocks of information – digested, soul-infused, energetic...Just upload the ready-made data, and it's done."

"Have you noticed that those we call geniuses are always paradoxical? They either radiate boundless energy or exude a strange, sweet, deathly tranquillity." Space paced the room.

"Everything has a price. The law of conservation of energy..."
Time waved a hand, brushed back his hair as if dispersing mist.
"Alright, let's go further, deeper – somewhere into the Middle Ages,
the age of witchcraft. Keep tracking that gene – 24-X-315."
"Or maybe we should check the dinosaurs?"
"Actually, that's an idea...Though I doubt it. That was an
entirely different stage, a different era on Earth. We deal with the
era of humans."
"Exactly..." Space pressed the keys. The computer whined softly
and lit up the night.

MONASTERY

An old, old monastery – solidly built, warm, reliable. Its underground chambers held barrels of wine, the scent of eternity, and
the primal pulse of hearts hidden beneath the hides of great beasts.
Torches flickered, casting shadows reminiscent of ancient cave fires.
Dim light, suspended time, compressed space. In the company of
others, one might feel a romantic solace here. But alone, one was
cosmically defenseless.
It was enough to drive a person mad – waking up on a bright,
windy morning only to realize they were alone in this vast and
towering fortress-monastery, where in its cellars, one might stumble
upon the rotted bones of martyrs of the faith, or of those who had
paid the price for an unruly, grueling earthly life.
It was a strange and terrifying sight – the trees growing atop
the monastery roof, witnessing young, strong orthodox Cossacks,
proud as oaks, being led into the damned, cavernous depths by
Jesuits, only to have molten lead poured down their throats, their
skin flayed from their bodies, or to be fed to the rats. And for what?
For their faith. For choosing a different path to reach Loa. A horror
beyond horrors.
Perhaps the greatest horror of all is when that which is meant
to bring peace becomes an instrument of destruction. That is
the true Paradox.

Two women spoke of this. In the old, old window of the cell, the Moon stood still – stained with fly specks, ensnared in the delicate trap of a silent spider. One woman was a fifty-year-old nun; the other, a refugee with two children. The year was 1914. The Great War. One could say that the Earth itself was spinning as a refugee.

The nun was ashen-faced, her eyes the color of quail eggs. A large – perhaps overly large, for a woman of her stature – nose glowed faintly with an extinguished, or rather, strangled, thirst. Like overripe pears splitting open between one's toes. The other woman was simply a woman. A peasant. She had grown from the earth itself. She had never attended school but had taught herself to read and write. She was not one to dwell on the Bible, unlike some… Like everyone else, she went to church. She perceived the world in the aching unity of all living things. She knew countless folktales, riddles, and proverbs – more than anyone could count. And she told them so soulfully, so masterfully. She never took money for it like those bloated professors did. And as for fame…

The nuns had taken her in, along with hundreds of other refugees, within their monastery walls. The men, meanwhile, had to guard the horses and their meager bundles outside, beneath the very walls of Christ's Brides. The women lay where they could – most often in corridors, within the service quarters.

And so, the sounds of horses snorting outside the monastery frequently blended with the deep, collective snores of the women sleeping in the cells. And through that chorus of snorts and snores, two voices murmured in quiet conversation – Sister Lyudmyla, the nun, and Hanna, the refugee.

"Above all else, sister, you must save your soul," the nun said, piously crossing herself. She picked at her nose, which, frankly, would hardly have pleased God if He were an aesthete. "Do you pray, sister? Do you pray? We are all steeped in terrible sins. Drenched in them."

"I turn to God, sister," Hanna replied. "I bow my head in prayer only at confession. But I always turn to Him. I don't ask for much. So as not to be disappointed."

"In Him?!" The nun's eyes flashed with something almost Jesuitical.

"I am a weak woman, sister."

"Oh, pray, pray! You are a dreadful sinner…"

"Well, you see… two children, a war, a husband…"

"All of it – earthly, fleeting. It tests us. There," she hissed, jabbing a finger towards the ceiling, where, in her mind, Heaven surely lay. "You know, even among nuns, there are different kinds. Oh, very different! Tell me, what kind of nun can she be if she's already not a maiden? There are those who can no longer have children. They indulged themselves, indulged and indulged – until they were practically oozing. And once they'd had their fill of life – straight here! But I, praise be to God, have made it to fifty, and –"

"But really," Hanna mused aloud, secretly crossing herself to stifle a laugh, "why would God want women who aren't maidens?"

At that moment, the door let out a dry, eerie creak. Some of the women stirred – perhaps even all of them. A shadow appeared in the darkness – clumsy, hunched. A child let out a sharp cry. Only a true woman could recognize the sound – a newborn, no more than ten or fifteen minutes old. Hanna curled into a ball.

"Oh, oh, oh." The nun whispered conspiratorially into Hanna's ear. "Do you know, do you know what this is?"

At that moment, Hanna's daughter, Tanya, woke and whimpered, asking to go to the toilet. Hanna sighed and began to rise.

"Listen!" The nun yanked at her sleeve. "This is something awful. Awful. One of our nuns has just given birth. That man… her lover… He came to take the child away. Ugh. You could say he practically delivered it himself. He wrapped that slimy, newborn flesh – and now… Where is he taking it?"

Hanna broke into a sweat. The words she had expected to come from her own lips stuck in her throat. The nun fidgeted beside her, and the two women, like shadows, slipped out into the courtyard.

A crimson moon. Still air.

The man placed the infant on the grass. It whimpered. He raised the shovel… but let it fall slowly beside the child. He spat to the side. He flipped the baby over, pressing its face into the dirt. He set his foot on its head. The cry became earth. Quickly, he dug a hole, placed the infant inside. Glancing around, he pulled the lid from a wine barrel used for communion. He laid it atop the child, dug a little more around it, and buried it with swift, generous motions.

The two women cowered, watching. The man did not see them – not because he didn't want to, but because he couldn't. He saw only his own soul. He was stubborn and silent, like barbed wire.

"Ohhh!" Hanna let out a primal moan. "People! People!"

The nun only yanked at her – Oh, you fool, you fool! Why would you?! – and pulled her head into her enormous hood, like a snail retreating into its shell, like the child-murderer shrinking into his own soul.

Like droplets through water, the monastery's windows began to flicker awake.

Hanna lunged forward, clawing at the dirt, unearthing the child. As the usual, easily imagined, harsh commotion of blame and accusation stirred, she already held the baby in her arms, licking the dirt from its tiny face like a mother dog – because it was still alive.

No one even noticed that on this very night, the Moon had gone into eclipse.

The human farce of justice was just beginning – who was the mother? Who was the monstrous man who had tried to kill the child he himself had conceived seven or nine months earlier?

The baby's mother – the nun – was a delicate, pale, fragile thing, with a heart that trembled like a gust of wind.

She had been sent to the monastery at fourteen. By fifteen and a half, she was already a mother.

Who had seduced her? No one knew.

The trial of the nuns, led by the old, righteous abbess, pried from her only this:

"He was an older man. I met him by the river, where I went to collect holy water. He told me he loved me, that he would take me away from the monastery, that he was wealthy… He kissed me – on my cheek, my lips, my neck, then… then everywhere. I remember… I don't remember anything. We met almost every day. And for the past two weeks, he had been staying in the monastery as a refugee. He loved me…"

"Who was he?" the judges hissed.

"I don't know. He was very silent… but very wise." The girl whispered with lips as fragile as glass.

A heavy silence fell.

The Council of Christ's Brides prepared to pass its judgment.

"Time, Time, quickly find me that silver-haired man. Who is he?" demanded the fiery Chance, addressing the dignified Time seated at the computer.

Time, silent and authoritative, pressed the necessary keys. The screen lit up with the words: "Such-and-such, professor at such-and-such European university."

"His guardian angel must be a drunkard," remarked the serious Fate. "A brilliant and talented man, yet he couldn't master a simple earthly craving. Passion clouded his reason – tender, like the blood of a dead tree."

"Don't turn it off, don't turn it off! I want to see how this human court judges those who loved with their bodies," pleaded Chance, who had arrived together with Fate.

"How would you judge them?" Space asked, narrowing his eyes.

"By Loa's point-based system, which is founded on love?" Chance clarified.

"On love of the soul, which leads to love of the body, not the other way around," Fate blushed. "There's no great mystery here. The girl is inexperienced, still a child in spirit. She grew up with her grandparents, no parents. When they died, kind people sent her to a convent. Her seducer isn't the devil, as humans like to say, but he failed to restrain himself. If he had truly loved her soul first and then come to love her body, it would be a different matter. But his sensor – his 'angel' – doesn't even emit the faintest glow. So, by Loa's measure, his love is nonexistent. The verdict is clear: erase him from the computer's memory as well. The girl, however, should be allowed to grow into herself. Who knows - she may even become a diamond one day."

"You've placed them correctly for the Final Judgment," Time chuckled into his fist.

"Yes, yes, but what will you do with them in this life, as Fate? After all, they're still alive. Especially the nun," Chance looked at Fate with the air of an examiner.

"Don't you see? Humans are deciding this themselves."

"And you don't want to intervene this time?" Chance pressed on.

"I do. I will act through that woman, Hanna – the one speaking with the long-nosed nun. As for the silver-haired seducer, I leave him to you, Chance. Feel free to drop a brick on his head – whether by human hands, the paws of beasts, or the fluttering wings of songbirds."

Fate pulled a remote communication device from her handbag – one linked to the computers of Time and Space, and now, even to Loa's Master Computer. She strode out of the Centre, either offended by the universe or resolute – as fate itself.

MONASTERY

Meanwhile, the people had no idea that Fate herself had intervened in the process, rendering them powerless to change anything – though they believed they were acting in the name of God. Some, particularly the ostentatiously devout, piously crossed themselves, recoiling from such a dreadful matter, while inwardly lamenting the passing of the days when such a bride of Christ could simply be burned at the stake, as their good old predecessors – the inquisitors – had done.

Hanna stepped forward. "Maybe I don't understand something, people. But to me, it seems this… Yes, this girl broke the monastery's rules. That's true. But she didn't break the laws of Life…"

"She has angered God! God Himself!" voices in the crowd cried out.

Hanna's face turned night-dark, as calm and resolute as an August night.

"If she has angered God, then let her answer to Him!" Hanna said. "But my heart tells me that one day, she will become a strong and kind person."

"Let her be whatever she wants – but outside the monastery." The abbess declared, her pale lips trembling. "Together with her bastard."

Hanna approached the young mother, took her by the hand, led her to her child – and together, they disappeared into the crowd.

LOA RESEARCH CENTRE

"So what happens to them now? Hanna has her own family," fretted Fate, sitting alone somewhere.

"Now, let them be." Chance replied over a special transmitter. "You've done your part. The genes – and I – will take care of the rest. In the General Computer's memory I've seen countless human embryos at the fish, amphibian, and mammalian stages of development. Priests, monks, adulterers – they've all destroyed them. Space and Time – or even Loa himself – immediately reintroduce some of them into the wombs of fertilized women as valuable (diamond-grade) material for future generations. They insert them, of course, at the genetic level. And lately, even I, Chance, have been allowed to intervene… as have you, Fate. We have democracy now. As for that nun, here's my advice, for old times' sake… Look into her soul, turn on the angel-sensor display. The newborn too has a romantic and restless soul. See how brightly it shines? 600 diamonds on the scale. Set them on a path toward a Romani camp. I've long since realized that impoverished freedom, after life's upheavals, is the best soil for growing diamonds."

"I'll think about it," Fate smiled, flexing, and shut off her personal computer.

A golden, windless rain of autumn leaves began to fall.

HANNA

Hanna sat on the worn wooden steps of a Russian log house, peeling potatoes – potatoes she and other refugee women had stolen, or rather, more accurately, gathered, from railway cars the night before. It was 1920… Hanna, her children, and her husband Herasym had seen and endured more than they could bear. Only yesterday, she had witnessed a Red Army soldier drag a Polish soldier out of a doghouse, dressed in nothing but his filthy, bloodstained underclothes.

"I am wounded! I am wounded!" the Pole pleaded.

And the Budyonny cavalryman sneered:

"Wounded for whom? For the lords? For the vermin?"

and with that, he struck the man across the head with his saber.

The Polish soldier could have been old enough to be his father.

Hanna had found a friend in an old Tatar woman, someone who radiated that rare, inexpressible domestic-heavenly calm – a wise, aged serenity that all people seem to know of, or at least sense, and perhaps, for which they live out their days. The two women quickly bonded. They worked hard, talked for hours, losing track of time. Perhaps they were happy. The children certainly were.

"Is it raining?" the Tatar woman creaked open the door.

"Yes, rains small-small," her soot-faced great-grandson mumbled.

A slow, sorrowful rain had indeed begun to fall. It made things feel warm and safe – safe in that fragile way only two women could understand. But beyond them, the unrelenting law of life persisted – struggle, or rather, its most extreme form – war. Animals devoured animals and plants; plants consumed insects (some, like Aldrovanda and bladderwort, even ate fish); humans ate everything, sometimes even each other. They killed one another for living space, for fate, for time, for mere chance…

As a blade clashes against metal in a lathe to shape it into something harmonious, so too did all things serve the production of Loa's ideal matter, through which he could realize his grand designs. And these designs? They were only left for humans to guess at. Loa had granted them only the ability to hypothesize. And he himself?
He simply smiled, it seemed.

"You know, Hanna," the old Tatar woman said, setting her knife to a potato. "A month ago, my ninety-year-old father passed away. I remember him. My children remember him. My grandchildren… perhaps. But my great-grandchildren? They won't. And my great-great-grandchildren won't even know he existed. That's where memory of a person ends. It's as if they never were…"

"That's just human memory," Hanna sighed deeply. "But up in the sky, or maybe somewhere beneath the earth, everything is recorded."

"People remember the great ones for thousands of years," the Tatar woman mused, gazing into the rain.

"But does that make it easier for them? Or harder? No one

knows. Maybe they rack up points somehow. But for or against them? Who knows?" Hanna scratched her temple with the handle of her knife. "We won't figure it out, sister. It's not given to us, to humans…"

"There's only one great truth we are given," the Tatar woman said. "We know we are finite. And we even have the power to choose when we die…"

"You know," Hanna interrupted, "back in my youth, when things were unbearably hard – everyone has those moments, when life feels unlivable – I suddenly had the simplest of thoughts: I could leave this life at any moment, if I wanted to. There are plenty of ways. But to return… at least in this form," she gestured toward her body, "I never could. Life is short as it is. So, we endure. And when it becomes too much to bear, just remind yourself that you could end it anytime – and suddenly, you feel strong again."

"At my age, there's another thought that brings comfort," the Tatar woman said. "You realize you no longer live for yourself, but for your children and grandchildren. You become a kind of vessel, their guardian angel." She glanced out at the downpour. "Look at that rain. Come, let's go inside. Tell me, what happened to that nun? Where is she now? I never got to hear the rest of it…"

"It still burns in me, but I was powerless to do anything…"

They tucked the children under the warm, smoky wings of the evening and bolted the door against the uncertain times. Any moment now, their husbands would return on the backs of their horses – from hunger, from ruin, from civil war.

All night, the two women of different nations communed through their souls. Hanna remembered the long-nosed righteous nun and told how, in the end, she had been forced to accept that the girl she had saved from the grasp of the Church had chosen to follow a Romani man and his camp.

"You can fight fate." They agreed. "You must. But to defeat it? That is not given to us…"

The women returned to their work.

Outside, the night grew damp. Even Fate itself did not dare to win.

The jangle of bridles rang through the dark.

LOA'S DIARY

1. Yesterday, I listened to the grass, the water lilies, the cries of seagulls, the ants… And yet, it is always humans, humans destroying everything… Or perhaps I am too self-absorbed. Maybe Nietzsche, that wild and demonized stork, was right – perhaps it truly is better if I die? Or set myself a more intriguing task – to create, instead of myself, a human-Loa, a diamond. Of course, maybe it was a mistake to have created humanity at all, and now even more so… But for this, it is worth existing! I will try. The mere mechanical combination and mixing of genes will lead nowhere good… Yet, ultimately, synthesizing the most creative minds – that is what I need. By elevating all of humanity to a higher informational level, I may be able to synthesize a diamond of the highest grade. What disturbs me most is all that is false – false preachers, false artists… Some of them shine so brightly that I had to develop a new computer program just to recognize them without error. One last time, I will attempt to create the God-Human. Christ was a brilliant attempt, but humanity was not yet ready. He acted as a powerful catalyst, but not for all.

Information! Information! Again – information. This is the greatest power.

2. Now, to specifics. Should it be a man or a woman? In the end, it does not matter, because I need a soul, not a body. I divided humanity into male and female only to create more paradoxical situations and thus – struggle. The energy of love is the most valuable thing. This mistake can no longer be undone, so whichever soul is most suitable, let that one be chosen. Although, perhaps, a woman has the advantage…

3. The defining criterion for a God-human is the ability to create living beings who could, one day, also build computers and, in time, become a Creator. After all, I do not know my own lineage. That is the greatest mystery. There are mysteries even beyond the gods… It all leads to a strange mathematical finality, and yet, an infinite continuation.

4. In the end, we are all – even the gods – a part of everything, and everything is a part of us. I was not mistaken when I sent Christ with the most essential commandment, the Law of Existence – LOVE.

Everything is One. Even more so, considering that, in reality, everything is ultimately immortal… Humanity does not realize that their souls are stored in the memory of non-human computers, which monitor every blink of their eyelashes. After bodily death, these computers evaluate the soul based on the Scale of Love – and either destroy it or use it as seed material for future life.

5. If humanity were to combine the truths of all religions, it would arrive at one true syncretic faith. Each complements the others perfectly, illuminating, even on the screens of human computers, the Primary Law of All Living Things – LOVE.

Everything proceeds as intended, and ultimately, comes to me.

6. And everything seems just. The soul of an ant crushed by a girl running to her mother is judged on the same scale as the soul of the girl's mother. And to whom more is given, more shall be asked… All souls are equal before the Law – whether of a thistle or a stork, a human or a horse, a swan or a crow…

7. Anti-Loa… Oh, how ridiculous humans are! But then again… laughter is what sets them apart from all else in the Earth-laboratory. Anti-Loa is everything that opposes God – or perhaps, in human terms, Loa's wife – Death. In reality… Each is both Anti-Loa and Loa, depending on which coordinate system one uses. For a slave-owner, Anti-Loa is a rebellion of slaves. But for the slaves, it is the slow-burning agony of building pyramids, stone dust clogging their throats. For the Internet, Anti-Loa is a hacker.

But ultimately, not a bad idea for a battle of souls against each other. That virus – that once rebellious angel-sensor – still wanders through the Living Computer of the World, making human souls tremble before the dark, the magical, and the unknown. Humans very rightly called it the Fallen Angel.

It is indeed dangerous for the world, but not for me, since I can destroy both it and the world together if I choose. For now, though, it is a brilliant mistake, one that will help me refine souls to divine purity.

The Satanic geniuses – they are black. Black diamonds.

Of course, this means there are fewer white ones, but the ones that remain – how pure they are! If they resist the temptation to turn black, if they withstand it – then they shine all the brighter. It is always easier to get dirty, to be tainted, than to pass through early springs and late autumns with a great and radiant soul, dressed in white.

The unclean power – it exists in all religions and human belief systems.

Paganism – perhaps the most intuitive, and therefore the most accurate – intertwined the sacred and the sinful, making gods of Wind, Earth, Fire, and Water, while its dark forces were everything that destroyed them.

And yet, conflicts exist even within these elements, which is the greatest paradox of all: water drowns fire, fire evaporates water… This is Death – or Anti-Loa.

And when such contradictions exist in this paradoxical unity, that is what Life truly is.

That is what grows diamonds.

Enough for today. How fitting – the ink in my pen has run dry…

LOA RESEARCH CENTRE

"It's a pity we can't read Loa's Diary." Space smirked slyly, rubbing his hands together, realizing a little too late that spitting on them in front of someone was almost like spitting in their face.

"Well, as the Bible says: 'Know me by my fruits.' Go on, take that same gene – 24-X-315 – and spin further." Said Time, restrained yet adventurous. "Come on, old friend, spin the wheels, stop it at some war where the presence of gene 24-X-315 is already recorded."

Space pressed a few keys, white as ivory or the sclera of a young eye. Dinosaurs roared, pterodactyls snapped their beaks, and terrified volcanoes spontaneously smoldered. The primal nature of Earth, through their throats, screamed out its wild yearning for reason, while Loa, still young in his experiments, had turned the planet into a laboratory – preparing it like an open cage for the arrival of delicate structures, hardening and testing it with the crude ones.

"See, on this level… There – two massive creatures are battling, as big as the launchpads of intergalactic spaceports. Gene 24-X-315 is nowhere to be found here yet. Some atoms are common, sure, but genes..." Space trailed off, scanning from bottom to top.

"Oh, we've tried everything already!" Time pressed a key himself. A bowstring twanged like a vibrating wire… and then the opposite. Warriors with hawk-like faces, mothers with the faces of seagulls, swords, beastly helmets, hunger, primitivism – the war of bodies, and only slightly of souls, and even less of minds. "A lot of 24-X-315 is already present here. But we need to spin further – to the extreme opposite."

On the screen, human history flickered by at the speed of a fast-forwarded film, its trajectory set to detect signs of 24-X-315's presence.

It wasn't hard to imagine how arrows transformed into bullets, bullets into more refined bullets… But what about souls? That's what intrigued Time and Space the most. They had only recently realized that, unbeknownst to themselves, they were growing diamonds of the soul. Intellectually, they understood that history had wars, but the film strip revealed a deeper truth – that wars were history itself – macro-history. The micro-history lay within the souls of plants, animals, and humans throughout those wars: how external fear influenced the internal fear of each potential diamond.

"Stop at the last world war." Space suggested casually. "No need to disturb long-dead souls before Judgment Day."

"Are you serious? I only work with pure memory. Resurrecting specific souls – that's something only Loa can do by pressing his special key, like that nuclear button for human presidents. Honestly, very few will be resurrected by the time of that so-called Judgment Day. All the dinosaurs are gone. A few humans might remain, maybe."

"And then what – another stage?" Space grew uneasy. "By the way – when exactly is this 'Judgment Day,' the end of the Human

Era?"

"When humans create a computer on Loa's level – when they can imbue bodies with souls...Wait, no, that's not quite right. When they successfully grow a god-human… Pure logic doesn't apply here. Maybe this entire experiment is a failure – maybe nothing will come of it. Christ was crucified, after all. And that was a real attempt, a real milestone… Well, here's your 24-X-315. All wars are the same."

"As you always say, you don't have to drink the whole barrel of wine to know its taste – a single sip is enough." Said Space. "So tell me, how do these 'brilliant genes' behave in war?"

"Brilliant genes or geniuses?" Time smiled wisely.

"We're tracking genes. And that's even more interesting – more elegant, wouldn't you say?" Space countered, launching the computer again.

In just five seconds, a millennium of human history unraveled before them, revealing itself in accelerated motion as nothing more than a continuous history of wars – which, in turn, contained the history of class struggles, tribal feuds, national conflicts, individual rivalries, all interwoven – humanity against itself, the soul against the body, molecule against molecule, atom against atom, nucleus against nucleus, proton against electron…

Yet despite all this, the dynamic equilibrium of the entire system remained intact – a precarious, critically thin balance on the edge. This was how diamonds were grown – souls forged by the divine paradox of concentrated energy, passing through temptation, depravity, and the demonic, as well as the brightest, most godly things – all while possessing formidable intelligence, wisdom, and depth of soul.

This fusion – this diamond – was, in other words, intuition.

Intuition is God plus Anti-Loa. The soul plus the body. The positive plus the negative. Intuition is paradox – the spark of life, from loneliness to love, and back again.

"Oh! Oh! Oh!" Time grabbed Space's hand. "This is it – stop here. The indicator light is on – 24-X-315 detected. Slow it down."

On the computer screen, a city from the early twentieth century emerged. A real city, because it breathed an old-fashioned air, the kind that created atmosphere – which, perhaps, was the very essence of art. Aged stairwells, timeworn windows, everything steeped in human history and the eternal imperfection of the cosmos itself. A sweet, stone-like calm, which – and this is the true horror of human existence – cannot last forever.

A living being must do something.

And when it is too weary to hang itself, it will be grateful when enemies arrive to do it for them.

This way, a person kills two birds with one stone – escaping peace into peace, moving from laziness into laziness.

In the end, only the truly strong can be truly weak – those who fear nothing in advance. They are ready for anything.

A STREET IN A CITY RESEMBLING LION'S CITY

A group of young men, at that age when swagger comes naturally, stepped out into the rainy evening streets from an ancient entrance hall in the city centre. For those with an artistic sensibility, the place smelled of something indefinable… For the townsfolk, it reeked of rats, old preserves, and coffin wood. Just as souls perceive ancient tombs differently, so too do they experience the old houses of old cities in their own way.

Among the group was one man in grandmother Hanna's family. He had ended up here out of curiosity, stopping by on his way home from Russia to Hrubieszów, Poland. He had met a local resident by chance on the train and decided to pay a visit… He was the one who carried the 24-X-315 gene. His name was Stepan.

The young men entered the park.

"You know, Petro," Stepan said to his new acquaintance, "I've always wanted to go to university, but my father would never allow it. The farm… acres of land. Still, I think I'll give it a try. To be honest, that's why I came here – to see if it's possible."

"I think I told you that my sister works there as an assistant in one of the departments." Petro responded with genuine enthusiasm. "You're an interesting person. I really want to show you something I wrote – a short story."

"Why do you write?" Stepan asked.

"Why do we live?"

"I think Schiller said it – one makes a mistake if they try to force their personal philosophy into their art, their worldview into their work. Do you want me to tell you the reasoning that's kept me alive all this time, kept me from hanging myself over the absurdity of it all? First, there are fundamental philosophical laws.

For me, there are four: Everything has a beginning and an end. Everything returns to its beginning – children and the elderly are alike. Extremes always turn into their opposites. The beginning is beyond our control, but the end – sometimes – is."

The group split into smaller groups, each following their own interests, but all moving toward the same destination: in the park, a world-famous hypnotist was set to perform, accompanied by his hunchbacked dwarf-clown – his wife. Petro had seen her just a few days earlier in a store, pushing a pram with a child inside. A bizarre spectacle. A strange, celestial chill passed through anyone who walked past her. Was the child also deformed? How had she, with her impossibly thin legs and fragile, twisted body, even given birth? And yet, inside the pram lay a large, rosy-cheeked, healthy-looking baby. Perhaps she had taken the child from an orphanage – abandoned by its "normal" parents. Or maybe… it simply wasn't hers. A relative's? A friend's?

The natural curiosity of people knew no bounds, lingering in the air.

"You have an interesting way of thinking, Stepan – like you've already finished university. Although… you were probably born with it." Petro said, almost to himself.

Stepan continued:

"You know, everyone is their own hypnotist to some degree. We may not have the self-sufficiency of cats, but we can at least convince ourselves that we have a soul, set our own rules for this game we call life."

The young men entered the park.

"There is something else I would like to tell you about hypnosis," Stepan turned to Petro and reached out his hand, as if to pull him closer.

Suddenly, a sharp shot rang out from somewhere nearby.
Everything scattered like shrapnel, uncontrolled and chaotic.
Stepan fell onto the golden leaves.
Dead.
Who? Why? For what?

No one ever found out.

In times of turmoil, in the diffuse, transitional moments of history, a human life – a name – takes on a strange, metaphysical glow.

Everyone simply decided it was a random incident – some idiot fooling around with a gun, firing into a crowd just for the hell of it.

"It was just his fate," Petro said, rubbing his eyes.

And that was it.

Stepan was buried somewhere, no one knew exactly where. To his relatives, he had simply vanished – and that was all...

LOA RESEARCH CENTRE

"You see, Space, what this love-struck couple has done!" said Time. "This time, Chance has clearly won."

"Why so definitive? If they love each other, then Fate can be coincidental, and Chance can be fateful... A high score is given to those whom both Chance and Fate 'love'." Concluded Time.

On the display screen, fields bathed in misty pink and golden morning light appeared, followed by explosions, corpses of flowers, animals, and people scattered all around. Then, evening fields again – cemeteries. German soldiers quartered in village houses, feeding chocolate to the children of their enemies. Some might find parallels: a rabbit doe gave birth to five kits and died; a young housewife, feeling pity, nursed the orphaned creatures with a bottle, dedicating three hours of her precious youth daily to them. Then, when everyone had long forgotten about it, she served stewed rabbit at a family celebration. Such is human mercy.

"Here's another one with the 24-X-315 gene. Mykola Romodan. See what a fine man he is – he could stop a horse at full gallop. There he is, a Banderite in a hideout. Then the Germans took him into the SS Galician Division. And here" – the reel spun a little further – "he's a Soviet machine gunner, marching along a road in Poland, wet with rain as a tongue, with his battalion...Oh, there, he's embracing someone – a fellow countryman! Neither of them is alive anymore. The one who survived the war died not long after. Mykola Romodan fell on the Oder, just a little before the war's end... His elderly parents later wanted to visit his grave in Germany, but their health and other rural concerns… well, you understand. Another Fate. He never married, never even fathered children on the side. All that remains is a portrait for relatives, whose children, in the end, no longer knew who he was – that handsome, eternally young man on the wall. Politics here is worth nothing. The person matters most."

"You know, Time, somewhere near the lands where Mykola's relatives are relocating, around 1985–1986 (I don't remember exactly), some nuclear disaster is scheduled. Seems like a power plant will explode. No one knows about it yet – except maybe some trees, some grass. But their silence is incomprehensible to humans."

* * *

Smoke rose from concentration camps, cows and horses bellowed at slaughterhouses, metal melted, bones sank into the earth – bones of lovers, traitors, murderers, the suffering. The souls of plants, animals, and people departed into eternal sleep, their deeds recorded, their usefulness in cultivating diamonds logged into Loa's General Computer according to a scale known only to him. Only the Computer determined the distribution of soul energy once bodies were dead. Some souls were reincarnated as animals, others as plants. Some were simply erased as harmful, unnecessary.

Souls of those born but who died moments later became angel-detectors – though not all, only those christened with a specific genetic code deemed valuable by Loa's program for creating the New Loa. The highest chances, of course, belonged to those who believed in God, even blindly. But the greatest chances lay with those who wanted to be God – like Shakespeare, like Christ, who called himself the Son of God. And perhaps, indeed, he had the right to do so.

"Look, look – another 24-X-315 gene!" Space suddenly exclaimed. "Mark it down. He seems to be keeping a diary. I love indulging in human philosophizing."

"Ah, yes," Time nodded. "The owner of this gene – a Ukrainian, a peasant. But, by the looks of it, an interesting one. Pull up his file."

A table of data flashed across the screen.

"See? He speaks German, Polish, Russian, and his native tongue. Reads and even writes in them," Space marveled. "Ah, here's his diary entry:

> 1. The 1920s. Once again, we failed to build our own state. We have no elite, no lords. Only sub-lords. Our 'noblemen' always had to serve someone – Poles, Turks, Muscovites, Austrians, Germans, Tatars. Our nobles are sycophants. The proudest genes could only survive in those who turned to nature, who surrendered their pride to the land. Certain peasants – these are Ukraine's true nobility, our lords, our princes. Such is the fate of stateless nations.

Even Mazepa and Khmelnytsky, both were impacted through by Polish statehood. Why are the Germans such a strong nation? Because what is the exception for us is the rule for them, and what is the rule for us is the exception for them. They passed through the era of knighthood – we did not. God gave us too fertile a land. Constantly guarding it drained the nation's male strength, gradually depriving it of its finest women, the most beautiful, the most desirable – taken by the hair, carried away to various harems, tents, manors, chambers. Our strongest men perished in battles, our weakest served the enemy.

A shortage of strong, proud individuals – this is our greatest curse. A Polish lady fled Lviv, her maid became the new lady, wearing the dress her mistress left behind in haste or pity, along with the gaudy, beautiful Catholic icons. And our foolish Orthodox Ukrainians, in their deep-rooted simplicity, pray to them because 'they look nice.'

> 2. But knowing the truth and living by the truth are two different things. Many understand a great deal, but affecting change at the genetic level takes generations – even in the best conditions. God grant that this is merely the calm before the storm, that our people might yet shine across the globe.

> 3. Ah, if only I were a strong individual. But no – I am neither fish nor fowl. Perhaps our grandchildren will be more remarkable, stronger than we are.'"

"Time, Time, we wanted to see war, to observe how 24-X-315 behaves…" Space ruffled his old-fashioned jeans.

"You see for yourself, war is essentially just accelerated life." Replied Time. "Everything else is just explosions of dead matter. But… observing souls in extreme circumstances – that is what's truly fascinating."

"But sometimes, creating those circumstances depends entirely on us."

"Yes, yes, and also on Fate and Chance. Keep watching." Time pressed a few buttons. "Look, according to Loa's program, if 24-X-315 is a potential diamond, Fate might make him miserable from birth – or take his mother away after a few years, like with Shevchenko, leaving him utterly alone, as alone as Loa itself. That is probably necessary. Fate devises the plan, and Chance finds the cause. From universal loneliness to universal love – and back again – is just one step. By the way, an interesting psychological point: remarkable individuals should ideally be raised by grandparents, or even great-grandparents, rather than parents. Personally, I don't believe in the upbringing of those with the genes of genius, but the atmosphere, the roots… those play a significant role. So, let's create extreme conditions for the gene we're following – 24-X-315."

"Alright, let's do it…"

Space and Time brewed hibiscus tea and settled comfortably into their swivel chairs. Meanwhile, Fate and Chance happened to meet in a beautiful city park. They tried to ignore each other but failed – and so they walked, they soared, above the autumn. What else could this be but love? What else? A bittersweet, overwhelming goodness enveloped them both. Not everyone in the universe gets to experience such a thing. The body melted into the spirit; neither time nor space, neither soul nor body – just pure energy of love, so lonely and so fatefully priceless to Loa, that even if this love had been stolen, adulterous, or otherwise forbidden, Loa's computer would not have taken notice. Love, it seems, recognizes only one law – Love. And that is why the most false phenomenon is counterfeit, non-fatal love. Like a tear streaked with perfumed eyeliner. A tear drawn by an onion. And yet – what a stark difference: materially, a tear shed over a lost love and a tear from a fly in the eye are indistinguishable, but the soul's work… The soul is the mirror of the world. And what is a mirror? In the end, it is simply night plus gold. That's the entire music.

"But, but, Space, look – 24-X-315 is gone from this… space. It's no longer displayed."

"Run a query."

"Running it now. Aha. Relocation due to political reasons. Operation 'Vistula'… Can you imagine how painful it must be for people, especially young families, to abandon their freshly built homes, their land, their ancestral graves – their spiritual estate? When a person is alone, it's easier. But when they have a family…"

"Not everyone has the same level of attachment to their home-land."

"That's true, not everyone." Time said, his voice heavy with thought. "For peasants, it's stronger. They are the most self-sufficient, the most natural people. They live like this: born from the earth – work the land – return to the earth, with proud and pure souls, without writhing and twisting through foreign cities like snakes. No professor could compare to some of these village elders…"

"Maybe – no false professors could?"

"No, Space. A person who aspired to become a professor is already incomplete, dependent, formal, even if they are highly intelligent. A professor serves people. A wise person serves Loa – and people… and animals, and plants, and stars… and for the eagle, and for the ox, and for the donkey, and for all creatures alike. And yet, many good people leave the village – to chase happiness, ranks… May God judge them. In the end, all people will leave the earth sooner or later. And the Earth, with a capital E, too."

"You know, Time, we're turning into quite the bores! Don't you think? We're rusting away!" Space turned on some lively dance music. "Here's your extreme conditions for souls. This is where they either harden or break."

"What do you see there? Aha. A penal army battalion, building a road through the taiga near Neta – in the hills. And there's the 24-X-315 gene. Well then, let's see. Let's go."

THE CAMP

Frost cracked the glass. Sparrows, frozen stiff, sat on the wires, falling asleep in place – then dropped, like dimmed stars, into snow as thin as a hymen. Winds from Chita – those sharp, dry "Chitinkas" – spun the earth. The taiga was Martian in its desolation, and yet, earthly and familiar.

Near the Buryat village of Ugdan, pale, milk-and-blood-coloured cows wandered naked. They were used to the frost...like they were to death – which, likely, they didn't even know existed. People know death exists – but not what it is. Same with frost. It is there, and yet you can't touch it. Something about it is unhuman. Self-contained cows. Masochistic soul-people. And here's the paradox: the more self-contained the animal, the more animal it is. The most fragile and human is the person shaken to the core, endlessly searching.

* * *

Here, in the taiga frost, you understand most fully what it means to be HUMAN...

...Men were cleaning their guns.

Later, as the taiga night dropped upon them, some were assigned to peel potatoes. Nobody wanted to...But Sergeant Dzhakharov – half-literate and performatively cruel – poked his finger mockingly at the chests of the most sensitive convict-soldiers. And yet, somewhere deep in the craggy, cave-like creases of his face – carved by a half-wild heart – there was a flicker of pain, and behind that pain, something fatherly, something protective. His animal-human self had landed precisely on the knife-edge – and held its balance. Which way it would tip depended on a draft through the barracks...or someone's chronic cough...or the whispering breath in the corner closet of the dilapidated barrack, where tough-looking Dagestanis banged swearing-drunk Buryat women, and the guitar meowed in the hands of the Russian Kheraskov, friend of the storekeeper, a crafty-looking Tajik, handsome in that universal way that anyone on Earth – of any nation – could understand. There were twenty-seven ethnicities in their company of this penal battalion.

And so – they went off to peel potatoes.

Every soul twitch of every man involved in that oddly familial, yet fatally survival-driven prison-army ritual was being recorded by the Loa Computer. What's the point of stealing information from the Computers of Loa, Time, and Space? If so, then all writers – engineers of the human soul – are nothing more than pirate-poachers. In this case, let's call the struggle of human against human and nature ethnic hazing. Fair enough, considering that character is, without doubt, shaped by geography. Unlike the well-known military hazing, this ethnic kind is particularly revealing – of a person through their ethnicity, and of an ethnicity through individual character.

In brief:

Are the laws of nature fundamentally more primary than moral ones – or not?

In extreme conditions, everything is revealed plainly. Stripped bare. Truthfully. Just as autumn strips the masks from trees and shrubs, so too do these raw, primal, greenhouse-less conditions strip them from people – until you can see their spines like crosses... wrote Subject 24-X-315 in his back pocket notebook. In the company: Azerbaijanis, Kazakhs, Kyrgyz, Buryats, Dagestanis, Tajiks, Karakalpaks, Yakuts, Udmurts – even a Korean, Li.

Among the Slavs: four Russians, two Belarusians, plus three Ukrainians.

God forbid anyone mess with the sniveling, sleepy newcomer of an Azerbaijani – the rest of the Azerbaijanis would jump in like one body to defend him: as though the left hand was defending a finger, or an eye, or the heart...The three Russians stuck together, close-knit. The Belarusians – each kept to himself. Ukrainians too: if they weren't being touched at the moment, they let it go, like starved children.

Of course, there are exceptions...

But observing the cohesion of, say, the Buryats – you feel it in your gut – the force of Genghis Khan, whose spirit, by the way, still hovers among their souls and calls them, calls them to ride west against the Slavs.

"One for all and all for one" for them is not some thief's slogan, nor a salon knight's creed – it's a law of blood. An ANT HILL.

Such nations had to be, are, or will become powerful states...

A nation, like a person, has childhood, youth, adulthood, old age...Fulfillment, as a rule, comes in youth-adulthood, not in old age.

Sometimes, it's during that moment that the nation is under the shadow or control of an older, stronger neighbor who still "wants to party" out of surplus energy – because their own house feels too small...

Then again – exceptions exist. Or rather, there are no rules: look at Banderite resistance, look at fierce independence struggles from a people so beautiful...and so servile...".

A sharp, dirty-snotted blow – sudden and strange, like coitus underwater – landed between his teeth and nose.

Something cracked. Stars burst into his eyes, slowly fading. One wish surged up in that inner starfall: that the soul wouldn't tear apart. So vast and defenseless it was – like the sky. Like the Universe.

– What the hell are you doing, you rat? Sitting pretty, huh? What're you scribbling? Snitching, are you? – barked the looming face of Tmutarakanov, the twenty-four-year-old company sergeant, with eyes wild and tender.

But it wasn't him who hit.

It was Private Fyodorov – toothless, bitter, vicious – mad, really.

– Go clean the latrine...– he caught his voice with his belly, spun it like a belly dancer, juggled it – and flung it far away from himself.

Because he was afraid...of it.

LOA RESEARCH CENTER

"Look at the soul's rough work, Space! We were right to engage the soul-maturing process under extreme conditions."

"Uh-huh." Nodded Space.

"A truly brave person is not the one hardened in the struggle for survival, not mentally ill… Recently, in the library, I saw a cat who amazed everyone with its unusually bold behavior – squeezing through the turnstile at full speed, walking straight toward gruff men without flinching. Turned out… he was blind. It was eerie and unsettling. So, I think truly brave beings are rarer than we believe."

"24-X-315 is still just a child. Why didn't Chance intervene then?"

"Because he's smart. Look, Space, what kind of thoughts are born in 24-X-315's mind when other beings are kicking him with their boots until blue blood seeps out – forcing him to do their physical labor by physical means. The very labor that, as we know, is the consequence of being expelled from Paradise… from the Creator's original laboratory."

The diamonds cracked. And maybe that's how it had to be. It's the simplest way to keep life going: put a rapist and a whore in the same hut. After all, a monk and a nun – if they're not fake… But a combination of a prostitute and a monk, or the reverse… There, the odds of birthing a God-like being rise by thousands, maybe billions of orders of magnitude.

"Skip ahead a bit, will you? I can't watch this sadism anymore – the "blood on the rocks" of the barrack's frozen floor, where it's always minus ten to minus fifteen degrees, since only the stoves are lit – the heating system froze solid."

Space once again pressed the keys on the piano of life. On the screen, as in some terrifyingly vivid film, biological bodies rustled into existence – what, according to Engels, constitutes life itself.

Kadyrov, the brutally steely and universally enraged plumber, hadn't slept for three nights. He was searching for the spot where the steam pipe had burst. He was freezing, his teeth chattering, yet carried out his work with Siberian grit… And he did it. Then he slept like a hero, and two days later he was already giving a concert as a soloist in the battalion's ensemble. He played with a fierce, icy flame. Almost everyone feared him.

"Want me to light up his true essence on the monitor, Space?"

"You, Time, clearly don't trust my intuition. It's obvious. A rare type, but still as far from the diamond the Creator seeks as we are, you and I."

"Let's move on… Oh! Stop!"

"The hills… the wild rosemary… Rawness and authenticity. Almost no diamonds here… But those few – undeniably real."

…Building a road in winter demanded fire, fire required wood, and the dry wood clinging to the hills needed people to cut it down, haul it away, place it on surfaces blasted clean of rocks and trees with dynamite – and light it. The fire thawed the permafrost, helping the people dig graves – like holes – on the left and right sides of what was not yet paved, but already traced by the first humans as a road through the taiga. A step to the left, a step to the right – an abyss filled with eternal roots and some kind of (also eternal, it seems) but broken and rusty water.

The animals merged with this tiny patch of Earth-globe into a seamless whole: hares ran, deer leapt with a flowing grace, bears dreamed in hedgehog-like curls. Sometimes, in the deeply primitive yet paradoxically cosy atmosphere of the taiga, a crudely hewn hut appears – deep green like dark blood – a womb. A paradise for the exhausted (and in the taiga, being light-hearted in body is impossible; as for the soul – hundreds of novels could speak to that.) To find such a hut in the forest at fifty below zero outside, and a hundred degrees below zero inside human hearts, while having a piece of bread and meat in your pocket, matches – was like being born in reverse – crawling back into the womb.

"You know, when death hovers over a person, when soul becomes body, and body becomes soul – and the whole thing becomes everything or nothing – the only fixed desire is to become a sperm again, an egg cell, or a fetus in a mother's womb, where it's damp, warm, and something alive throbs above you – maybe your mother's heart, maybe God… It makes no difference. That's the real comfort. That's what sperm longs for, the Universe longs for, and likely God too." Said Time, and added, "Look, 24-X-315 is having these exact thoughts. And not just thinking them – he's materializing them. There he is, with another guy – Baybekov – dragging a log, barely managing it. 24-X-315 has a piece of bread in his pocket, all his thoughts fixated on it – he's starving, utterly drained. But psychologically, all he wants is to be a squirrel, tucked into a warm mossy hollow. He craves milk, a big, big quart of milk cold as snow-bound silence, and bread – white and warm, like the udder of the kindest cow in the world."

"But Time," Space fluttered, "even with all this, not even our computer picks up the neuronal connections that lead 24-X-315 to pull that piece of bread from his pocket and offer it to Oleg Bay-bekov: 'Eat. You're turning blue.' And he himself feels like hell."

"The thing is, Space, that's the kind of thing that can't be fixed – like Spirit, Intuition, Loa. It's of diamond order. Not matter, not spirit, but their joint product – spark, God, in a word. Thoughts in

the subject's head – those, yes, we can track. But from them alone
you'll never define guilt or innocence. You have to consider the
situation."

"Absolutely. A thought born at the cosy desk of some old fart of
a professor is not the same as one born at the existential edge
between life and death, in truly combat conditions, not just
'as close as possible' to them… So…"

The screen lit up: "I want to hang myself… That means I'm
human. I can still smile picturing myself dangling from a branch –
looking dumb and twitchy… That means I'm not a machine.
Animals don't kill themselves knowingly. And they don't laugh.
Though they do cry… Well, even if I hang myself:

a) Life's short anyway – you can leave it any time in any way,
but you can't come back (at least not in this human form). That
thought alone – that I can do it whenever I want, that it's my first
and last freedom – is what saves me. You see: a moment equals
eternity, and eternity – a moment.

b) Feelings lead to death, reason to life. Though if feelings are
all spilled out, that too is death (like Byron's ninety-year-old body
at thirty-seven – burned out physically because of the spiritual
intensity). Reason plus feeling plus music (wind) equals poetry –
which helps one live and die not as a mass, but as a human being…
Poetry is a sacrifice not to Death, but to Life…"

"Interesting. Let's see… what does this same person think
in a hothouse setting?" rasped Time.

*"That's three years later," said Space, lifting the phone
receiver. "Hello? Sorry, Time – (into the receiver)… Chance?
Okay, we're waiting for you. (To Time.) Here, read 24-X-315's
worldview directly from his mind."*

*"The paradox is that generally passive Eastern philosophy be-
came more like real politics than the outwardly active Western philosophy, which always opposes politics. Philosophy rarely addresses
the Creator choosing some people and not others. For all their
similarities, say, Socrates and Skovoroda – only the latter made
no distinction between rich and poor… Socrates' 'good' is known
only to aristocrats, the idle. Why are they the chosen ones?*

With dialectics, Socrates also brought irony – a state between laughter and tears, between pessimism and optimism, between science and religion.

Take this formula: philosophy = science + religion. If the Tree of Knowledge of Good and Evil really grew, there'd be only science. If man could create man, there'd be no philosophy either – or it would be pure science. But in reality, philosophy = Robot + Something. That 'Something' – eternally elusive.

That 'Something' is what we all search for. The Bible, I think, only has God and Man. Animals are brought as sacrifice… I disagree. Something's wrong! Search, search, and search again.

It clearly doesn't contradict Loa's design – since he made me like this.

What misfortunes does this life even have! The fact that I was born – out of some million-billion probability, that that exact sperm – mine – met that egg – that's the greatest gift from Fate, Chance, Space, Time, Loa, ultimately. So many unborn wait in line. Will they ever come to see, to feel, to smell, to love this world?

God, I'm divinely grateful to You that I am! That I was! Here… And now that I was – the rest is between You and me, me and myself, and this world. Forgive me when I'm arrogantly confident, and pity me when I'm timid and gentle, little and defenseless – for I am a little bit of You, and You – a little bit of me… Grass does not grow down… it either dries up, or grows – to the sky."

"There's nothing to do but keep silent." Said Time.

And silence fell.

CHANCE AND FATE

Chance was rushing – flying – to a coffee-conversation with Time and Space…When suddenly – coming toward him – Fate.

He had long ago sworn himself, with a vow hard as diamond, never to meet her again – that proud, capricious, eternally youthful and untouched-pure being, like wisdom itself, like happiness…

Moreover, the celestial Law of Life forbade them from being together.

But an unspeakable, terrifying force drew them to one another, looked through their eyes, moved their hearts, rang out like a high-voltage string at the slightest touch.

LOVE

The Loa computer had programmed forgiveness for all sins committed in the name of this energy – this energy so desperately necessary for the creation of a new God. And at the same time, the greatest hypocrisy was also born of this feeling.

Loa hated only one thing more than all else: FALSEHOOD.

To detect it, to track it through Time and Space, the most sophisticated programs were created – for falseness was always most rampant where it had no business being at all: in art, in love, in friendship – in everything that binds the world together for the sake of God.

And the greatest falsehood was betrayal of God in the name of the Anti-Angel, who was especially fond of meddling in these very domains – buying up souls, those closest to diamond-purity, in exchange for human glory, money, love.

And yet, LOA had not immediately destroyed one of his archangels – so that he might become the final frontier, the inspector of true and false essence in diamond-souls.

Because the line was so thin, so nearly invisible on the highest registers – whether a soul was truly divine, or a pseudo-diamond, just coal...

And so, the rainbow that rose between Fate and Chance could not have been satanic. Loa's Programme would simply annihilate Chance and Fate – and even Space and Time – if they sold even a fingernail, a pinky, to Satan.

They knew that. That was the guarantee.

But as for self-interest...Even Loa himself probably wasn't immune to that – because rest for the subject is already a form of falseness. A soul may slip not just to zero but into negative registers, especially after soaring at impossibly high speeds, on the edge of madness…

There was no gain in the love between Fate and Chance. On the contrary – there was lawful prohibition, a sentence waiting to be passed...

But when everyone suspects, senses that the love is real – envy is born. And if it is very real, very strong, and blindingly bright – what emerges is a silent blessing.

There was no point in deception between Fate and Chance. They both understood: in this Universe, everything must be paid for. The only question is – who pays? And at the very Time when they burned for one another, became a single knot of divine energy – someone among people, or animals, or plants, desperately needed their presence, their intervention, their help…

Someone cursed Fate, someone prayed to God for a better one, someone swore at a black cat that had accidentally crossed the road just as a bus driver was passing – the cat was rushing to meet a white she-cat – and the driver was carrying thirty passengers, and at home he had five kids, and each of those passengers had their own Fate, their own loved ones, small children...

This entire simply complicated and complicatedly simple Machine of the Universe-Loa kept spinning and spinning for the sake of growing a certain number of diamonds – who, fusing into a fiery invisible tangle of sentient awareness, would become the New God, or alternatively, would help sustain the Eternal God, the one that human beings can vaguely imagine or iconify.

We are not granted the ability to "imagine" infinity – that is, the finiteness of infinity.

That's not for us… hallo? – into the far… far… far...– that's all there is.

Only the "low beams of consciousness" are switched on…

Meanwhile, Fate and Chance floated through heavenly-earthly parks, afraid even to brush pinkies – because the spark that arose from a single touch gave birth to entire worlds – Galaxies.

It was unbearably heavy and blissful for them both…

"You know, Fate – turns out happiness is the hardest thing to endure." Said Chance.

"I feel that too." Fate whispered with her eyelashes straight into Chance's eyes-soul.

"I won't last long at this altitude! I have no right to say it to you… Beloved."

Chance understood nothing – but felt everything, on a universal scale.

"Don't look at me like that!"

"And you don't like it?"

"I love it – so don't look at me!"

"So what, what shall we do…?"

The whisper turned leaf-starry, wave-like, salty, real…

A flash of a white glove – and they were no longer together.

Because Fate was bound by duty – Loa was waiting for her.

And Chance had just been on the phone with Space and Time, arranging their meeting.

Such is life.

Such vanity.

Such drama.

Such joy-pain.

"Only the very strong can allow themselves to be very weak," Loa wrote in his Diary, and added:

"Chance and Fate still need to gain a little more strength, a little more height, so they're not afraid of falling.

Falling – with hope for ascent – that is what we call HAPPINESS."

LOA RESEARCH CENTER

Space and Time had just had lunch – finished off the cake left over from yesterday's birthday – and now sat in heavy silence. Words were unnecessary. This feeling-sensation often overtakes creatively self-sufficient entities of the Universe. Especially now, as another screen displayed a scene: they were burying a woman-academic who had died suddenly, at the height of her strength, from breast cancer. Her fellow scientists stood grey-haired and diverse at the edge of the grave; one of them was speaking – reading from a sheet the list of her merits, titles, and so on. The words, one could feel, were as unnecessary now as they were to her present body. Off to the side, two dogs were mating.

A young man, trying to scare them off quietly and discreetly, only made things worse – they locked together and began howling in pain, dragging each other in opposite directions. The absurdity of bodily existence, compounded with formal achievements, was so stark that it gave off a feeling of eerie discomfort – a sense that you yourself were being buried along with the deceased, with that woman who had not long ago been beautiful.

Time, what do we have there on our main computer? – asked Space.

Pretty much the same as over there, – Time pointed at the funeral. – Suicide by coat hanger, lice-ridden soldiers shaving their privates, sodomy between men in a closed system – the prison-army...In short, the dark side of existence, the grinding of diamonds through battle with nature and with other stones (far from diamonds – or fake ones). That's how it is.

Look, look, Space, a library. On red calico, in big white letters, a slogan: "You won't read everything, but you must strive to." The company political officer, Tuksumakov Nurlanbek, is wetting a rag to quickly wipe off the chalked-in parody under it – matching in shape, content, and essence: "You won't fuck everyone, but you must strive to." Time scratched behind his ear. There's a deep philosophy in those words. Truly unhappy are the ones who can't hold themselves back and become slaves to Knowledge, to Love, to Fame, to Wealth… These are things a human can never have enough of. And perhaps true human wisdom lies in tasting from all these cups – even drinking from them – but not becoming drunk on any one, not becoming an alcoholic...

We've gone deep into philosophy again, old man. Look how that song in the gear room is bringing the soldiers' souls together. They sing to a guitar – and off they go, flying...

I'd rather stay silent about songs in captivity, Time replied. And so they truly did fall silent, watching – fragment by fragment, like film editors – another life-film-reel of a group of human-dots, among whom was 24-X-315, with genes that (according to the computer and their intuition) were potentially diamond – paradoxically childlike, strong, sinful and saintly all at once, the kind that sparkled with intuition...

THE CAMP

In the corners of the barracks-huts, jaws and ribs were being broken, the weak in spirit were being taken by force in every orifice, frostbitten fingers, ears, and noses were falling off...Parcels from home were eaten, letters from parents and lovers were read, memories of cradle-bound childhood were recalled and cherished... Some saved their soul and body (through the soul) with cruelty, some with weakness, some with songs, some with poetry, mumbling it by heart, extracting it from the brain and filtering it through the soul like oblivion, like a drug. It helped, because it made time pass faster – and, as we know, at high speeds in space, time slows down... thought moves fastest of all, and so time records the most (the inner, soul-time), while external (general) time accelerates accordingly.

From the cosmos, souls emerge eternally young, for the velocity of the soul is infinitely great.

For those who survived winter in the taiga, spring is celestial. Pure, ringing, cool. Lemon-windy sunlight and pink rhododendron. The white blossom of the rhododendron ("bahno", as we call it) is very rare – whoever finds it will be happy...It's something between a fern flower and a five-petaled lilac bloom...

In the morning you walk through the spring taiga as if among great stars, the air – like in the age of the dinosaurs. It's glorious if you are free and rich; it's terrible if you are a slave – to other people, to nature, to an illness, to yourself, to your own fear, and so on.

THE DIARY OF LOA

In such conditions it becomes vividly clear that the human being is a social creature. A good example – Shakespeare's King Lear. I created an ignoble being… Lear was a hero when he had his army, his guards, his servants… his title! But after his daughters betrayed him, and he sat out in a stormy field, half-naked, defenseless and unarmed, he could just as well have been eaten by a wolf, for example… The frog had burrowed into its hole, the mouse too… All animals and plants rely for protection only on what I – Nature – gave them. They are NOBLE. A human, however, faces a tiger, say, armed with a powerful rifle, dressed in the pelt of that tiger's mate, well-fed, well-protected – and calls himself a hero! But strip the man down, as the tiger is naked, take away the rifle (as the tiger has none), and behold what he really is – MAN – a pitiful King Lear in the wilderness… He has nothing to counter nature with. He, like all of HUMANKIND, is IGNOBLE. Every day humanity kills millions of animals. But if a dog somewhere bites a human, or a horse escapes from a circus or a zoo and kicks a guard to death – the news will flood nearly every media outlet in the world, like a fever.

Shakespeare depicted well a King Lear who feels his own insignificance before the world of nature and the world as such – when he is no longer a King but simply a human being: the most repulsive and (sometimes) the most divine of creatures. And it is this divinity within the repulsive that interests me… a flower growing from a pile of manure… The soul-diamond. Though this is more Hamlet than Lear, of course. Hamlet… the seeker, the doubter… creaking, ringing… "I must be cruel, only to be kind…"

So then, Shakespeare. King Lear:

LEAR: "Thou hadst little wit in thy bald crown when thou gav'st thy golden one away… Is man no more than this? Consider him well… Thou owest the worm no silk, the beast no hide, the sheep no wool, the cat no perfume… Thou art the thing itself: unaccommodated man is no more but such a poor, bare, forked animal as thou art… Off, off you lendings! Come unbutton here." (He tears off his clothes.)

Loa picked up the phone: with thought, he connected to Time and Space, inquiring about news of the experiment. He asked them to transfer their file to his computer. They did.

On the screen was winter – with 24-X-315, who was at times smashing frozen excrement with a crowbar, and at times, spitting out shards of his own teeth mixed with blood, refusing to submit to the demands of the tough, brazen, and miserable soldier-cons. He stayed obstinately, painfully, profoundly silent, responding only with a quiet chest-smile to the cons' card games, where the wager was to force 24-X-315 to curse – to break him, in other words… But no matter what, he remained unmoved. Within him, like the seed of a fetus, music was developing – a music that was God.

That's why it would have been easier to kill 24-X-315 physically than to force him to kill that music within himself – a music that, for some reason, feared profanity. And the more it feared vulgarity, the less 24-X-315 himself feared anything – as a living human being. At that time, he belonged to the category of people who are ready to die at any second… because there are still those who are ready every minute, others every hour, or day, or lifetime… and then there are those who fear death to death itself… Hence, the scale of spiritual strength in a person. Animal strength is of a different order, since it only senses death intuitively – perhaps in the same way that a human senses God.

So, Loa took 24-X-315 into his own hands. There was simply too much resemblance between them. He began, invisibly, arranging moments and opportunities for him to compose music – scribbled onto slips labelled "Combat Bulletin." This music he sent to his relatives back in his forest homeland. The letters with music, of course, were screened by local security, who pathetically tried to decipher the notes and treble clef using the squeaky-leaden key of their sickly statist-convict curiosity – and all they found was nothing, zero, zilch… The naïvely childlike and yet powerful symptom of 24-X-315 bypassed police traps in an adventurously non-adventurous way, and so was even more dangerously subversive – and infuriated the dull and narrow-minded: "Look at this pest… sly to the point of being… unsly, cunning to the point of simplicity, secretive to the point of disarming openness…"

"I'll issue a command to Fate and Chance to arrange a meeting between 24-X-315 and Satan. This diamond deserves the ultimate test. If he withstands even that without selling out, he'll make fine material for God…" – Loa wrote in his Diary and dialed the coordinates of the love-struck pair – Chance and Fate… He – a substance of the utmost unity of word and deed – as the critical threshold of all genius – GOD, in a word.

FATE AND CHANCE

The tide of their love would rise, swelling toward its highest crest – when everything, damn it all, seemed worth abandoning –

then fall again, into a void so bleak and spiteful that it too demanded the same. Somewhere deep down, they both secretly craved those times when they shared a burning, common purpose – given to them by Time, by Space, or, on rare occasions… by Him.

This time it was Him.

They had grown hungry for real work again – the kind that alone could hush their salt-sweet, ache-sharp, orgasm-bitter, black-and-white, quietly-ringing unsayable longing that kept asking every nerve of their souls: if this isn't love, then what is?

The task: discreetly arrange a meeting between 24-X-315 and the Prince of Darkness.

Fate and Chance leapt into action, eager, almost gleeful. They were together, united by one remarkably strange, thrilling and yet romantic idea.

"So… how do we go about this?" Chance asked, chewing his gum with the air of someone deeply immersed in business.

"Quite simply." Fate replied. She was, at times, terrifyingly brilliant. "24-X-315, being an Artist at the core of his being, wants to taste everything. So, despite the fact that his spirit has already come of age, we must guide him toward attempting suicide...out of curiosity."

"True. And that's exactly the kind of moment when some Beelzebub might take an interest in a subject like this – after all, his computer's not a bad match for Loa's. I bet a warning light blinks when someone like that hits a threshold… or maybe a sound goes off – cutting through the black light of the infinite." Said Chance thoughtfully. "So, really… this one's a matter of… chance."

"Well then – show me what you've got." Fate cooed, spinning coyly away without saying goodbye.

Why is it always like this with her… from unbearable tenderness to that smug indifference – just a breath between the two. Exhausting. Fire melts ice. But ice… splinters fire. Chance thought with his heart. He clenched his fists, ground his teeth, spat with frustration – and went off to do his part.

Love had already done its own.

Ivan Puzach, his toe fractured down to the bone, had begun to hang himself.

Anti-loa drifted near. "Should I tempt him with clichés – to make him one of mine? No. I'm too proud for that. Not from just any piece of shit. Loa will destroy him anyway…But what if there's still hope for a Kingdom of Satan, after all? If I gather enough of the right material…Here begins the truest choice, the deepest drama. What difference does it make? God or Anti-Loa. God, the original? Without Satan, after all, you can't make a proper God…"

ANTI-LOA

In the infirmary of the taiga military unit – the Camp – Belarusian Ivan Puzach was carrying a heavy bucket of water and…broke his big toe. It had been frostbitten once, but it no longer looked black – just normal. Turned out the bone inside had rotted through and snapped.

24-X-315 was closest to Puzach, and felt it in his spine, like a jolt of electricity.

Outside the infirmary window, the chief of staff and his deputy were carrying past a goat that had been shot with an automatic rifle. An orgy was anticipated. How else could one stay sane in this place without going completely off the rails?

A call came from the barracks: a letter had arrived for 24-X-315. Some kind soul had even brought it.

The news was unkind: his grandmother had died.

A swarm of purple-coloured thoughts stirred in 24-X-315's mind:

"In the year 1092, during Nativity Fast, plague took 7000 souls in Kyiv. And how many died in endless wars – most of all from steppe invasions…"

That was from a book so old, it may as well have been time itself.

"A man wins a car in the lottery – suddenly believes in God…"

An absurdity of existence spun through his mind like a flower market – bright, chaotic – and dripped drop by drop, like birch sap, into his heart.

"Why do babies die in earthquakes, crushed under falling buildings? They're angels, after all! So – an individual life means nothing? Do as you please, what's morality even worth anymore? In the end, entire species vanish. The aurochs, for example…"

24-X-315 rose in spiritual revolt.

And where there's proud spiritual rebellion, there begins Anti-Loa – who is, after all, none other than the proud Arch-Spirit who once claimed his independence.

But, created by God, he could not be stronger than God.

Otherwise, Loa himself would be flawed and unwise.

"But then again… humans have created machines millions of times stronger than they are physically, and computers that surpass them intellectually...It is only in spiritual strength that humans remain unmatched among animals – just as Loa stands unmatched among humans. Loa, for the sake of growth and struggle, took a genius-level risk: he created angels, knowing full well it would lead to rebellion. But rebellion is life. Loa must have understood that without Satan as his counterforce, he too would be mortal – unable to produce a sufficient reserve of diamond souls for self-replacement, for renewal...in short: for the creation of the New God. Without Satan, God is finite. With Satan, there are two outcomes: either Anti-Loa destroys him, or he delivers tested SOULS-DIAMONDS, forged in the true fire..."

So thought 24-X-315, as he found a medical strap, tied it to a pipe above the nurse's door (she wasn't in), and began to hang himself. His soul and body were ripe for this. Something unworldly stirred...

And then – like the clanging of a hellish chain – a thought rang out:

"Humans are cancer on the body of the Earth. They'll destroy it – along with all animals, all plant life...In that case: Hitler was the most divine being – because he destroyed the most humans..."

No. That's a satanic being. The Creator doesn't need quantity and quality. He needs quality of quantity. Without people, Loa would perish. But Anti-Loa wants to destroy humanity, God's creation, to become God himself and craft his own kingdom, his own material.

Sure, there's the option of swaying people to his side – but reaching into filth?

No. The real thrill is stealing diamonds from God, right from under his… well, from under his nose, so to speak – those mature, fearless, pure diamonds of spirit and creativity who are at peace with DEATH, just as one might be with one's conscience…

Such thoughts rushed over 24-X-315 like a neural storm as he slipped the loop around his neck.

But that was theory – skeletal theory, bare, like a Christmas tree at the end of the season.

The practical thought was simpler, stronger: I can always do this tomorrow… or whenever. There's no way back. So I'll endure.

Suicide hadn't been part of the Creator's plan.

Then again, nothing was absolute: not all suicides became Satan's property – far from it.

That decision belonged to the computer, or in this case, to Loa himself – through Chance and Fate.

"Well, well. Why not? You really like being with the Old Man? Look at his servants – the clergy: fat, stupid, smug. With me, you'll be a proud rebel. And one day, you can rise up against me too – or against Loa – once I switch on your high-beam consciousness. Go on – hang yourself. Fall into the dark light of my tangled wings," breathed the Prince of Darkness from above and below.

And then, once more, a piercingly simple – therefore genius – thought struck 24-X-315:

"I respect rebellion, wildly so. But I respect RISK even more. And Loa was first. He's OLDER. In his youth, he was a rebel too…"

"So am I taking a risk," laughed Anti-Loa straight into his great soul, as if laughing from inside it. "The souls I recruit – they too can rise up and overthrow me!"

"If that's the case," said 24-X-315, "then why would I join someone who's asking? I'm a rebel by nature – maybe I should stand against Loa directly, like you.

You're proud. But Loa is NOBLE. He doesn't call out – he gives freedom to choose."

"He doesn't call? Then what do you call the billions of temple priests and artists acting as go-betweens in all the world's religions?"

Anti-Loa, it seemed, was right about everything.

And yet something within 24-X-315 resisted.

It was like an iron tree rooted in his spine, flowering in his skull, bearing a single apple-shaped thought:

Go to Loa – or rise, as a Human, against them both –Anti-Loa and Loa.

Anti-Loa read the thought and said:

"You won't manage it. You're an ant without high-beam consciousness. And that light – only the Old Man or I can grant.

It comes after death. But the choice of whom to follow must be made in life – especially right before death. And by the way, the MYSTERY is revealed only to the chosen, even after death. That's how the central computers have it...So…"

The former archangel kept talking.

"You tempted Christ. He didn't fall. I feel closer to him, somehow, than to you. And that's that." Nearly shouted 24-X-315.

"They crucified him. And how do you know where he is now? You doubt everything. And here I offer something concrete.

Maybe – maybe this betrayal is what Loa actually wants!

He split humanity into sexes, didn't he? Just to make life harder. You could've self-fertilized otherwise. Instead, you have to go through soul-wrenching labor just to...screw someone."

"You're not wrong. But...I'd rather rise up against peers – or younger, stronger ones. Loa, as you call him, is the Old Man. And old age – my soul tells me – is to be respected.

Beating up an old man isn't heroism. But standing up to a young Loa? Maybe I'd do that. I'm a proud man. But I see Loa as a grandfather. I pity him. Respect him. Love him."

"You can be logical too, it seems. Very well – watch yourself..." The Lord of Darkness laughed again – genuinely, tenderly.

The infirmary door slammed open. 24-X-315 instinctively yanked the cord off and returned, like a current snapping back into the wire, to circumstance.

When the nurse entered – a stately woman with eyes unnaturally blue – he was already standing there, arms outstretched:

"I really need a piece of paper...Please forgive me for coming in uninvited...Your daughter is beautiful..."

He murmured something like that, not even hearing himself, caught between Eternity and Vanity.

The nurse chuckled sweetly, pretended not to notice anything.

But the next day she discharged him from the infirmary. As she handed over the papers, she looked into his eyes and asked:

"Do you think God exists?"

"Yes. Absolutely," he answered.

"Prove it," she said, in a voice one could only imagine.

24-X-315 had the feeling Satan's temptation hadn't ended.

"Prove he doesn't..." he replied – and with a push of soul-body will, he shut the door behind him.

But his brain – his computer-head – kept working.

Or maybe it wasn't a computer. Maybe it was Anti-Loa still posing his questions – brazen as life:

Where was Christ between the ages of twelve and thirty? Maybe he was a thief. Maybe he'd already had his fill – of women, of wine...

Why, if he preached love, did he never take a woman?

Why only male disciples – unjust.

Was he perhaps...deviant, toward men?

And besides – scientifically, historically – it's never been proven that he ROSE AGAIN. In the flesh. In this world...

The questions were sharp. And to the spiritually mature 24-X-315, they felt like natural extensions of his own inner life – grateful, worthy ground for contemplation, testing, struggle.

HE NO LONGER FEARED DEATH, for he understood now:

He is death – if he chooses to be – at any moment. For himself and for others.

...It's harder to be God: he cares not just for people, but for animals, for plants, for every cell...

Anti-Loa only lurks – waiting for the best of humanity...

That final thought fizzled in 24-X-315's mind like a spent match – and just then, the chief of staff appeared.

The day was cold and bright.

"Pack up, old man. Orders from Moscow. You're getting discharged... So, let's go." Said the grizzled Afghan veteran, patting him on the shoulder.

"This will be better." Chance said joyfully. "Fate had to step in, because I'd already done everything I could."

And he ran off to find his Fate.

"Well done, Chance." Said Fate. "I honestly didn't expect such a delicate, precise job from you. You arranged everything perfectly for 24-X-315."

Fate kissed Chance on the cheek.

They both blushed.

"And in the end," Chance gathered himself, "you wrapped it up beautifully too. I think Loa will be pleased…"

Chance, a bit timidly, took Fate by the hand – and just then, Loa summoned them. He was writing in his Diary:

"24-X-315 held fast. Now, ahead of him, alive, lies the greatest trial: long, drawn-out, sharp – the battle with himself. Self-polishing. That's the hardest. The only salvation, the only path – is faith in Me and in the Spirit, in the GOD-SONG. He's already generating immense energy for Me. Very well, let him now try another form of the world – free creativity among those like himself. Diamond polishing diamond. I will lead him by the hand into the great city of his people – a curious city."

Loa praised Fate and Chance. He gave them more secret instructions.

They could barely contain the HAPPINESS they felt – for themselves, for 24-X-315, for Loa.

And off they flew, flew, dreaming…

24-X-315 was being sent off. The Siberia-hardened men… wept.

For good reason: it was this kind of human that Dostoevsky had truly loved (as Nietzsche once noted).

They – the convicts – were, deep down, in the permafrost of their souls, the most human of humans.

They gave 24-X-315 a new cap, boots, a coat… a belt.

They kissed him, and some wept – with terrible, masculine, brutal tears.

Even those who had hated him – wept.

From that day on, for the rest of his life, 24-X-315 loved people… divinely.

The officers drove him to the airport themselves.

KALI

Since then, the tenderness in 24-X-315 had not died, had not faded, it did not shed off like water from a goose – but now there was also steel in him.

He had become strong and bare, like a sword.

He seemed to have turned into a MEDIUM. The deep past and the distant future fused within him. The present became just a backdrop, something he no longer feared – something he ruled over, even in the darkest moments of his life.

Strong and bare, like a sword, and as sensitive as a tear on the blade...

That's how 24-X-315 arrived in Kali.

He had meant, had planned, to go to a different, more Slavic, sunlit city – but the cold-hungry magnetism of a woman from Kali subtly and stubbornly lured him in.

The city was exotic, bourgeois, tedious, beautiful, spiritual, ancient and young – like stone.

And like water wearing down stone, it slowly wore away even the strongest of divine souls.

It snapped, like cigarettes, the spiritual spines of those who had never broken, not even in the zones or in the frost.

TO BE TESTED BY HAPPINESS – IS THE GREATEST TEST OF ALL.

Superhuman happiness is a superhuman ordeal, for FAME is a sliver of the divine, a sliver of eternity graciously tossed down to humankind by the Creator.

Byron added to fame also LOVE, TRAVEL, WEALTH.

After drinking himself sick from all three barrels, a person burns out, loses interest in BEING on a physiological level (when the thirty-seven-year-old Byron was cut open after death, his heart, liver, and brain were those of a ninety-year-old – this despite the chosen one of God, as they say, had not been an abuser of alcohol or tobacco).

The spiritual whirlwind toward the starry heavens – flown with a broken moral compass – had done its work.

It would be logical here to add WORK to the list, but fire was born to burn.

That is, the human – if they are a bearer of strong Spirit – is condemned to the labor of that Spirit.

Spirit cannot not work. To force the Spirit to stop working, one would have to expend… an unknowable amount of energy.

Or rather, we do know it: you'd have to kill the person physically.

Otherwise, it is absurd to say of a LORD OF SPIRIT (like Ivan Franko): "He was incredibly hardworking."

That's the same as saying that the elements of nature are… diligent.

TIME AND SPACE

You see, Time it looks like Loa has decided to handle our test subject 24-X-315 himself, – said Space, adjusting the sharpness on the monitor.

Yeah. Now all we can do is observe and learn.

A light flicker of irony, soft as the light of the daytime Moon, passed over Time's gray-childlike face.

Loa had arranged for 24-X-315 to be tested by the city.

And that was after he'd already, so to speak, made it through Satan.

Women, Fame, Travel, and Money might still do their part, – Space stretched out slyly, with a slow gleam in his tone.

Well, we'll see...

Are Fate and Chance still involved in this one, or is Loa handling full self-service now? – asked Space.

I think they're still in it, but behind the scenes. Otherwise the life of a soul-diamond being polished would feel too unreal.

True...

Time and Space began reviewing fragments of 24-X-315's life in Kali.

KALI

"The Spirit feels worst where it is hardest to tell Good from Evil. In a Dionysian pageant of endless carnival, nearly everyone is in a mask – masks so deeply fused to the skin that only the divine eye can discern the soul beneath the face. Yet those souls are also the most exposed, the most defenseless. At carnivals, you must wear a mask. To be bare is a mask to others, but a fatal wound to oneself. The spiritual-psychological energy released in such exposure is a treasure to Loa. The battle between Good and Evil is, in the end, the tension between the FALSE and the TRUE.

Anyone can tell sausage from shit. But the higher the realm, the finer the line. A true diamond is nearly indistinguishable from a faux one – only the finest jeweler can tell, and the supreme jeweler is Loa.

The city is a great ancient vessel where falsehood and truth swirl in mad confusion. The soul-diamond, the Artist, the ultra-sensitive string of a being, the true creator must sift through the muck to find a diamond – condense it, polish it with himself (for only a diamond can polish another diamond), and present it to the Creator. The shavings and dust from this polishing become gifts for others.

Kali was full of dust and shards, which is why it was considered the spiritual Piedmont of a NATION OF POETS – a nation striving with all its might to become like America, though in essence it was not a BOURGEOIS, but a POET, with all that this entails. And perhaps its tragedy was this desire to:

a) seem older than it was;

b) seem worse than it was.

Psychologically, it's simple: if you can't change yourself through hatred, try love. Poetic love – the real kind, not the graphomaniac version..."

24-X-315 crumpled and tore this page from his "Diary", walked out into the evening park, and lit it on fire. Fire was a RITUAL for 24-X-315. Fire was sacred. Fire was FREEDOM. Everything else – including fame – was addiction.

"Why don't you tell people that you are a genius?" a Jewish
musician asked him in Russian. "If I feel like a genius, why should
I hide it? False modesty is for people afraid of themselves. And
posthumous fame, well...Bah! I say you should do more self-
promotion. We could even launch a joint bid for the Nobel..."

At first, 24-X-315 could only respond with an ironic smile –
as defense. But the words began to sow thoughts, doubts. In this
city of ants, this bustling mound, there was too much anti-art, too
many hollow drums booming loud, false, yet powerful, making
a show of it all. And so the doubts began.

He started to realize, somewhere in his gut: TALENT is not
a person's achievement – what matters is what they do with it.
Whether they sell out or not. Selling out is betrayal.

"Oleh, imagine a great long field, ending in a precipice, a chasm.
You can picture thousands walking across it, some taking hundreds,
even thousands of steps. Dozens stand already on the very edge.
And only a rare few make one more step – formally like all the
others, but in essence...That step is given only to GENIUSES. But
'to whom much is given, much will be required...' Maybe it's true
that Loa torments his chosen ones, bites them. Horses bite and kick
their favorites too, they say," declared the musician Ostap Shablii
to his friend – the talented stage designer Oleh Romodan – over a
bottle of blood-coloured wine in some smoky, pretentious Kali
basement.

"A..." was all Oleh said.

"I get you, man." Answered Shablii. "All thinking people
eventually reach that beautiful silence. There's nothing worse than
old chatterboxes and decrepit bastards. But when development is
artificially cut off, that's no good either. This ant-heap of a life,
this NEAR LIGHT OF CONSCIOUSNESS – God, it gets on your
nerves. But what can you do? The greatest wisdom is to accept..."

"Yes," said Romodan. "But you still have to live through everything..."

"Of course. If you got married as a twenty-year-old kid – liter-
ally and figuratively – your infidelity to your wife means one thing.
But if you married at thirty, having lived through dozens of girls,
it's something else entirely."

Creative people live as long as they're curious.

"Agreed," Oleh drained his glass, "but there's still duty – to the kids, for example."

"In theory, sure. But then why does Pushkin go to a duel? Mayakovsky shoots himself, Yesenin hangs...So many cases. No one can carry too much divine joy. A person is physically incapable of holding too much of God." Shablii muttered feverishly, like a prayer.

And then he caught eyes with her – hellishly beautiful, thin as a frayed string of black light. A Girl. The glance burned like sliding bare skin across knots in that string. In a flash, he felt male. She, too, instinctively, innocently animal, moved toward him. But physically, she remained somewhere in the Palaeozoic. In the blood of both, pure blue-eyed dinosaurs roared and hungered for scent and taste.

Artist Romodan caught the bioelectric spark between Ostap and the girl, pointed at his watch dramatically, excused himself, and slipped away. Ostap and the Girl were grateful. That alone united them already.

She approached – gliding through the room almost beyond the physical, the way they probably walk in paradise – and asked for a light. Ostap's hands trembled beyond control, as it happens sometimes...

He wanted to. And that unseen force that only visited him in life's most pivotal moments carried him again toward ACT.

She was slight and fluid, wearing a loose white sweater and snug dark pants that clung to her moonbeam legs. She radiated something soft, tender, minty – and at the same time glassy and sharp. Her hair was transparent, night-sea dark, almost maternal.

"That's how naked statues and mannequins arouse." Thought Shablii. Perfect. The rarest moment: when an act requires no soul-energy. It was all unfolding lightly, simply...

Red lips – the touch of cold ice – and fingers sparkling with icy fire...Swan down with glass shards – that was the Girl.

They WERE in an old art studio, one of the oldest corners of Kali. She refused wine. She seemed like an innocent priestess, earthly longing, a drop of cosmic love.

Shablii felt silly, wild. He was swept away. When she took matters into her hands – her white dove underwear, her bra, her glance, her knees like droplets of stardust pattering on otherworldly wine – Shablii fixed on one thought:

"HOW STRONG YOU MUST BE TO...ALLOW YOURSELF TO BE WEAK!"

He tried to outwit himself as best he could.

Something sticky and fragrant spilled over his stomach and above and below...It was the wine – no, it was her drinking and drinking and drinking...him. It was DIVINE.

Ringing in his ears, pressure rising from his gut to his chest. The ultimate weightlessness, and the deepest descent – to Earth's very core. Heaven and hell at once.

"Relax...just relax..." she whispered, a fern blossom rustling in the wind of breath, scattering everything into blue tufts...

Flickering in his vision like worn icons in a drunk village cantor's eyes, the outlines of his wife and children flared as sparks of ancient wood.

I sin to know God...I sin to know God...

That was his own phrase, scraped against him like a struck match.

The vast Emptiness of this Girl-Woman was small, slender, beautiful – she emitted butterfly tenderness (her lips were like a white butterfly's pink mouth) and primordial, unbridled dinosaur power.

Such a forging would shatter not just steel – but probably a diamond too.

It was an ACT OF WILD TENDERNESS.

SPACE AND TIME

"Listen, old friend!" Space was breathing heavily. "Why is the column on the Spiritual Energy scale so low? After all, we're witnessing an Event."

"Take a look at the DIAMOND SCALE." Time wiped the dust from it.

"Whoa!"

"The Diamond Scale is a paradox, a spark, the energy of personality being polished. As for pure Spiritual and pure Physical energies, I'll pull up the file for you. The story is connected to 24-X-315's colleague and godfather (Ostap Shablii). Here, look."

Time pressed a few keys. A face appeared on the monitor – Kolia Vorobel, a fervently altruistic, delicate, irresponsibly industrious soul, a literary editor by profession. Physically stooped, yet upright like a poplar in spirit, he had recognized Shablii the moment Ostap arrived in Kali and helped him however he could: introducing him to various circles, acquainting him with interesting people he already knew...dragging him through forests and mountains.

Possessed, unloved even in his thirties, Kolia once (by chance) met a woman in a library – and he took off. Not from uncontrollable passion, but from Love...

The exchange of greetings and flowers was charged with such an inner flight that his pupils – his inner Universe – dilated, his smile turned to tears, and the tears smiled...

Her name was Oksana Halayda. Intelligent, not young, self-burnt, freedom-loving. She wisely sensed Kolia's feelings – and directly, provocatively, yet femininely, offered him physical love... The boy, caught off guard and afraid to defile what he perceived as divine in this Woman, awkwardly refused, steering the conversation, as they say, in a different direction. She smiled with her whole body, swiftly cast off her readiness – and left for a nearby Big City.

He cracked. A rare kind of True Spiritual Love merged inside him with myriad natural, social, and cultural COMPLEXES – and pushed him deep within himself. The bottom he reached catapulted him upward. Fed by monasteries (where he spent his nights) and stars of solitude, he set off for the Big City. From Kali – to the Big City. 600 kilometers. Fleeing from himself and catching up to himself – at the same time...

On roads well-trodden and wild, the moral law within moved forward. Above him, a September sky, strewn with stars. Possessed by LOVE – this physically small, skinny man wore through three pairs of shoes, slept in fields and haystacks, survived on corn cobs, wild pears, whatever he could find. He spent nights beside kurgan stelae – the dwellings of ancestral spirits. To those stone women, he was already a MAN – but to himself, not yet. And to Her? It's not hard to guess what raged in his soul – though not everyone is able to understand.

He reached the Old Great City of his people. Slept on the grave
of one of his nation's ancient knights, which lay on the bank of the
Great River, bathed in the morning dew, called Her, arranged
a meeting on the central Square – and set off there on foot.

In a track suit pitted with stardust from the Milky Way,
unshaven, emaciated after fifteen days of travel, he bought a plastic
bag of grapes, a white, prickly rose – long, like the Road...

She arrived – with someone else.

It was cruel and wise. One nail drives out another. Love –
drives out hatred, hatred – love...But this is the hardest path...

He smiled – and took the train back to Kali. She was ALONE,
she was burnt out, she wanted nothing. He was scorched by the ash-
es. He blackened himself with her. He ended up in a hospital with a
psychological breakdown. He had committed a SPIRITUAL ACT...

"You see, Space, what a high level of Spirituality this man
possesses." Said Time.

"Then why not a high level of Diamondness?"

"A rhetorical question. Don't you feel it?"

"In this case – no. This person is a Loa-Artist of a high register.
He not only unites Word and Deed...he doesn't scatter words at all.
He performs spiritual feats through his physical body – at its ex-
pense (as is almost always the case)." Space replied without pause.

"You know, Space, to be honest – I don't know either. Maybe
our scale is flawed. Maybe Loa has hidden this KNOWLEDGE
even from us." Time grabbed his hair.

"Or maybe the answer is quite simple: Kolia Vorobel did this
for the sake of Love for a Woman...not for God..."

"He lies who says he loves God but hates his neighbor." So goes
the divine Word in the human Book. Love is the very essence of
God. LOVE HAS NO LAWS. LOVE IS THE LAW. Here, look
at this next file." Time pulled up the next fragment – a piece of
human life – on the monitor.

Her name is Svitlana Harmash. A sweet, strikingly pretty girl
with two ponytails sticking out in different directions. She grew up –
nearly ripened – on the wild, easy shore of a forest lake, naïve
and strong like the forgotten gods of the ancestors.

There she is, seventeen, rushing into marriage... Then, eight months later, giving birth to a little blond-haired boy. Then off to Siberia on a romantic work adventure. Someone's rainy, windy wedding… Dancing on vodka – like twigs drifting on water… A rugged Siberian soul, solitary and rough, wolf-like in his aloofness. Svitlana dances with him – hot, sensual, young as milk, tight-strung like the yearning of the universe. A flash, like a sabre-moon, flared between them – and everything rumbled. Deeply. Heavily. Irrevocably. And then it all flew, it all rang out.

They were both already strong enough to be worthy of love, strong enough to be weak and defenseless – like the sky on earth and the Earth in sky-Universe… There they run, salty and desiring… some hay appears… they ache for each other to the point of crying out; shivers, sobs, Oh God! The ultimate finality of everything.

This was the moment of the Universe's creation, like the eyes of a black stork with perfectly round suns for pupils in its centre. "Maybe, in those pupils, too, there are Mars' and Saturns, Venus' and Earths, where beings live...they just haven't invented the microscopes yet to see them. Infinity in the micro, infinity in the macro. And what is it, really? It's not for us to know!" A million times Ivan Volkov spun that thought-combination in his head-computer, and a million times he felt, with the healthy fibers of his soul and body, that what mattered most was what had happened between them – between him, a father of two sons, a friend to his wife – and this young girl.

He had been hardened, scorched, seasoned, but here… Dry logs, after all, catch fire quicker than those full of sap.

It was LOVE. The external laws of Christian morality – as understood by hypocrites and menopausal impotents – were shaken, stirred, broken to their very core.

What Loa's computer illuminated in this case, by what scale of sinfulness or sanctity it judged Svitlana Harmash and Ivan Volkov – even Space and Time didn't know. Nor did Chance or Fate, nor the guardian angels. And yet people long to believe in the burning-cold HIGHER JUSTICE of the ultimate LAW – that of LOVE.

"What happened next? What became of them?" Space grabbed old Time's hand.

"Fragments… You can guess for yourself what people like

Svitlana Harmash – childlike-sage natures – are capable of, and what they are. Everything, as they say, snowballed from there… Here, watch another fragment." And Time switched to another human on the screen.

Lada Pidhiryanka. Like Christ, she was at odds with her closest family, and by twenty had left even her mother. She writes excellent poetry, sings beautifully, organizes soulful-spiritual life in Kali. She lives everywhere and nowhere, open to all like a string, and at the same time closed, like an untouched string, like the still-sleeping voice of a string.

She kept flying and flying… Until one day, she had a child by someone no one knows. She refuses on principle to register a marriage, doesn't want to. Whether out of defiance to herself or to the world – who knows. She has plenty of milk, and she lives. She lives…

"Ah, Time, I've had enough of your fiery flying women." Space grumbled (somewhere at that moment, earthquakes happened, new worlds or creatures may have been born – or died – indifferent on some level). "Their scales are all too different to judge. Let Loa sort them out. I don't understand anything any more. I'm exhausted. Who's a saint? Who's a sinner? Who's soulful? Who's high-spirited? Who's a diamond, who's dung? Who's mortal, who's immortal? All of it is recorded in Loa's computer. We're PLAYERS, just like people…"

"Indeed, Space." Replied Time. "So let's really play. You know what? –" Time smiled slyly. "Let's transplant the genes of a few past geniuses into modern bodies and see how they behave in a faster, different kind of time. Let's see how the crowd responds – and the few."

"But no one will recognize them, Time. And if they claim to be Christs or Buddhas or Napoleons, they'll just be locked away in madhouses, psychiatric wards, and the like. Even in the most democratic societies." Space added sweetly.

"They'll have entirely different names. Though their appearance might, at times, give them away… In Kali, for example, there lives a composer – fairly well known – who carries the genes of Beethoven, and a poet with the genes of Byron and Lermontov (divine engineering allows for the mixing of qualities). Shevchenko has died again…

All art (as Aristotle said) is imitation. Every Great Artist started with imitation, but not all broke free from it...

And in the end, why cloak in secrecy those things which even people already suspect? We are Space and Time, after all! Look there – advertisements are posted everywhere: 'A meeting with Mozart and Alexander the Great at the opera house.' People DON'T BELIEVE. The relatively sane will be thrown in the loony bin, others – old maids, unhinged researchers of parallel worlds, and the like – are themselves straight out of the madhouse. A minority. The result? Fake."

"But surely someone will truly feel the presence of genius, if it's not a game but real?"

"Someone will. But to trust your won feelings is the hardest. And besides, who said people have to take this LIFE seriously?

Why not see it as a GAME? Skovoroda, Pushkin, Schiller, Shakespeare… In the end, it's all relative. Childlike. Everyone cherishes their OWN above all… The more concentrated the charge of the shell, the more expansive, generous the explosion…

Here, listen in – two potential geniuses are having a conversation in a late-night dive called 'Theatrical Café.'"

Time and Space changed the file.

A CONVERSATION IN THE TAVERN

The two of them were earthy – like a stallion's seed on rose pollen, like a convict's aching song before an altar. Noble in restraint, stubborn, and naturally disheveled. So different, they bordered on the identical. One was Ostap Shablii, the other Dmytro Bykovskyi. They'd been around – spiritually, existentially. Both lazy and Sisyphean, losers and Cossacks, misers and magnanimous souls, sowers of spiritual seed. They sat with firm resolve, sipping something, smoking, philosophizing. Outwardly calm, inwardly torn to the edge of divine profanity. They had known each other a long time – seen much together – not friends exactly, just old university mates.

They sat, drawing theory from practice: remember that one, that thing… why that way and not another… why another and not that?

"Why do we torture ourselves, living not like Americans? We are a NATION OF POETS. We live as such. And that suits us. We're chaotic, elemental. But that's who WE are. Paradise, I'm sure, will be Ukrainian, not German," Dmytro began, gazing far beyond the pirate-patched walls. "We have those exceptions, the misfits. They suffer. And then they have people like us. They suffer too…"

"Yes… What matters is affinity. And not being afraid to be yourself every second. Eternity is made up of moments. And whoever seizes even one moment completely – owns eternity. So it seems to me…" Shablii exhaled with the smoke.

"And what's more – discerning the real from the fake. Take this. Artists now – plentiful as manure. But a true poet is rare, like a hypnotist. He puts a person under – yet can't explain the mystery of his gift, not even to himself, let alone teach it."

"But gimmickry, spectacle – often outshines true talent. A genius composer would rather sit with notes, with his instrument, creating music, than promote it after the fact. Though that doesn't mean the more gifted you are, the more reclusive. Extremes are always diseased – they paradoxically switch poles, morph into their oppo-sites. There are no formulas – but intuition offers clues. Picture this." Said Shablii, gesturing with his hands to aid the tongue, that weapon of soul and mind. "Two yogis onstage. Both perform a levitation act. One of them invents invisible cords – strong, elastic, undetectable. He floats easily, smiling, high above. Thunderous applause, bouquets rain down – reward for his 'suffering,' so to speak.

The other yogi trains for twenty years – studies the laws of the universe, of the body, of dew and starlight. He floats too – but lower, less showy, sweating, bloodied lips. His MIRACLE is real. But the crowd came for spectacle, not truth… Sure, some people can tell fake from genuine – but they're unlikely to spoil the illusion, disappoint the crowd. And why should they? People want rest, not torment. THEY WANT A SHOW, NOT THE TRUTH. Truth is eternal. A show is a moment. That's the difference between false and true – for me."

"Which yogi would you choose, Dmytro?"

Dmytro Bykovskyi smiled pensively. "You're right. Real artists – like real hypnotists – are rare. You can't really learn it… not to the degree that operates in the higher registers. I agree with you: 'So many clever men – but no true wonder-workers…'"

"There's another thing." Ostap continued. "Talent is no personal merit. It's from up there." He pointed to the sky. "But what you do with it – that's the person's choice. Very few remain uncorrupted – not sold for cheap glory, for stinking, bloodstained money. VERY FEW UNSOLD AMONG THE TALENTED."

"But I think only the soul can be sold. The spirit is immortal – if it exists." Dmytro snapped a cigarette.

"The nobility of the artist lies in writing more words than he speaks. The same for notes, for paint… People pray to a silent volcano – but flee the one that erupts."

"I don't believe there should be any boundaries for genius… I don't think there are any. Truth is what IS. No point overthinking!" Bykovskyi cursed softly from the depths of his vast heart. "And as for falseness – Christ, in Scripture, came to unmask the hypocrisy of the scribes, the Pharisees – their pompous, showy piety…"

"Oh, yes!" Shablii stood. "But now they've made an idol, a fetish out of Jesus. His so-called priests have turned him into the very thing he rose against – he, the genius rebel, brilliant, like a… diamond. Oh, the eternal spiritual paradox – humanity advancing through denial of denial. Buddha, Muhammad, Christ become idols…and hundreds of lesser gods too. The world becomes pagan again, only now the idols aren't Perun or Dazhboh, but Christ and Buddha – filtered, crucified, commercialized. Mankind merges – economically, digitally, spiritually… What's next? Who the hell knows?" He cursed again, in the primordial, mucous-and-blood dialect of his distant forefathers' enemies – Turks, Tatars.

The question was blood: would Shablii curse hard if truly provoked? Cons, lowlifes – they tried to push him. In vain. Lately, he sensed he'd physically softened – or maybe become a truer artist – more fragile, more attuned. He'd mutter "sh…t" or "oh, mother of…" Not angry – more like talking to himself. Who knows?

"As for falseness – it's about outer vs. inner effect. A tear can be wrung from the eye by pulling a nose hair – or slicing an onion. But it can also fall for a star's descent. Feel the difference? To Loa, what matters is SPIRITUAL WORK, not physical or bodily."

"Uh-huh. Then what does a woman give birth to – body or soul?" Ostap asked himself aloud.

"If the child is born alive – Soul-Body. If not… well, it's clear."

"And when does the soul appear in the womb?"

"I think, right after sperm meets egg."

"Makes sense. They say even in early abortions the fetus recoils from the scalpel."

"What's your view on the death penalty for severe crimes?" Dmytro asked out of nowhere.

"Hmm… I've long feared giving myself an answer. The question is – has humanity, or any of its communities, matured enough for such humanism? Too many edge cases. If someone told me: whatever you say, that's what will happen – I'd say: 'I oppose all judgment of man by man. It's absurd… We'll all stand – maybe not all, but many – before the Higher Judge. And His verdict may be the opposite of the human one.' You know, there's this Polissian legend: Christ was walking with his disciples down a harsh road. A rich man passed by in a fine carriage – they asked for a lift, but no dice. Then came a poor peasant in a half-dead nag. They asked again – he took them in.

'How will you reward this poor man, Lord?' Peter asked.

'Tomorrow, his nag will die.' Christ replied.

'Oh God!' Peter was stunned.

'The thing is, God loves not only the poor – but their tears…'"

"Well, what do you think of that paradoxical truth, Dmytro?" Ostap asked.

"All truths are paradoxes. Let's just drink. In vino veritas! Truth is in wine. All this jabber – it's just HYPOTHESES!"

They drank heavily. Arms around each other, singing "There stands a high mountain," they stumbled through the streets of evening Singapore, greeting familiar women and men. They felt like the lords of Life.

Though that feeling, too, was false – fueled by drink…

"You know what, old man," mumbled Bykovskyi, "a woman gives birth to a soul. We don't see the reverse happening."

"Ah, what's there to say. All our thoughts – they're human, not divine. And all our deeds – human. Humanity, damn it, is

GOVERNED by the most natural instincts: sex, the hunt, even LOVE… That's where all this destruction, rot, and nonsense comes from. Enough. Let's keep singing."

And they did: "Youth will not return—will not return again…"

FATE AND CHANCE

"Ah, hello, hello!" Fate couldn't pretend not to notice Chance. Silence fell.

The hopeless pause needed rescuing – with a careless smile or the standard excuse: "Sorry, I'm in a terrible rush…" maybe a tap on the wrist where no watch was worn…

"Oh, we've become so frenzied… frenzied beyond reason… That's just how it is. An incapacity for action. Only verbal triumphs."

"It was easy for Christ to combine word and deed. He only had Himself to answer for. Not even children – at thirty, imagine… He had nothing to lose."

"Many have nothing to lose…"

"That's true, but…"

Fate summoned the volcanic force to bite her tongue and took Chance by the hand. He seemed to swallow himself – and gave himself over to Fate. They drifted through waist-high celestial grasses, scented with pure cosmos – and cosmos with them. They slept in a haystack of the Universe. They were gripped by a blissful crisis. They couldn't manage themselves, had entirely forgotten the people gathering for rallies, divvying up churches between denominations, priests beating priests over the head with crucifixes, politicians swollen with ego, too blind to see how laughable they were – instantly or by degrees.

Yesterday's swaggering, slobbering Ukrainian Communist party bosses now tear their clothes open to show traditional embroidered shirts – look how patriotic we are… And tomorrow (God forbid!) the Germans arrive, and they'll lick their boots with equal if not greater zeal… and confess: "Well, we weren't prophets, were we…"

Priests pampered by "proper" families, with their meaty hands and lips, will hear the confessions of old women pure as tears and girls untouched even by sacred grasses… before retreating to their plush, three-storey homes with two Mercedes in the garage – built by their devout flocks. Their bodies radiate peace, but their eyes…

Thank God, there are exceptions. The Spirit rests upon them. Paradoxical exceptions: sinful, at times terribly flawed. But holy. These EXCEPTIONS are often poor parents, poor everything – but they are GREAT. Nations, humanity, the Creator need them.

…Such images and conclusions glowed on the screens of Fate's and Chance's computers. They rushed headlong to aid one DIAMOND or another – and fell into despair. Then bloomed again. Kissed and wept.

Suddenly, a face loomed over them like an axe. It was Despair…

"Ah, to hell with it all! To hell with everything!" Absurd! Nonsense!

This was an uprising. A breakdown of control. A human being stepped outside herself, into the world that had, in fact, driven her out of herself. It was rebellion within rebellion. A storm in the soul of the Universe, and the Universe in the soul of the storm.

"To hang myself, to drink myself numb, to disappear, be gone!" – a young woman smashed windows, tore through everything and everyone around her.

"Chance, Chance! Look at her! That beauty's lost her mind!" Fate whispered, half intimately.

"She's not capable of losing her mind completely." Answered Chance, who had for a very long time maintained equilibrium and was blissfully surprised by the fact. "That's Halya. She's just had an abortion. A bohemian painter, a musician too. Just a beautiful, slender woman. Lives with some interesting guy in an attic some-where in the backstreets of old good Kali."

"Everyone thinks she's such an artistic lady… and in part, that's true, but something tells me she lacks that force, that real power that separates a true Artist from the lovely day-and-night butterflies who, in the end, burn up in the light of that STRONG SPIRIT Loa calls DIAMOND." Said Fate aloud, with her deep, beautiful eyes-Universes.

"Let's roll back Halya's timeline." Chance clicked his computer. "Ah yes. Smart girl. Came from the provinces. Wants to understand everything – spiritually, emotionally, physically. Got into university, timidly slept with the first bold, clever guy who 'screwed her and fell asleep,' but, obsessed with art, she barely noticed. Were it not for music, the soul's flying music, she would've suffered far more. Art has this rare gift – to let you live everything in advance: joy, sorrow, tragedy – it induces a mediumistic state… Here's Halya pregnant… Here's her wild struggle: to give birth or devote herself entirely to art… Here, with a cosmic act of will, she chooses abortion, borrowing twenty dollars from a friend for the operation… And here she is after a premature labor… Nearly lost her mind." Chance held Fate's hand tightly and tenderly, in a gesture full of mystery and meaning.

Fate fell silent.

"She could've brought a new soul into the world but traded it for the work of her own soul. The Universe's balance didn't suffer much. The soul – an alloy of her close genetic traits – returned to Loa's Computer, unrealized, its tiny body decaying or burning to ash – becoming earth, Earth."

"But people still can't agree – is abortion a sin or not?" Chance smiled sadly.

"Oh God. Sin… what a relative, idiotic notion! Isn't it clear that the foundation of all Being is Love? Nothing is sin in the name of Love. Everything is sin in the name of Glory, Money, etc. Simple as music."

"So – if a woman has an abortion for the sake of her love of art, it's not a sin?" Chance teased, playing the know-it-all.

"You can work it out with this simple logic: say the woman who has the abortion is a diamond – a spiritually powerful being. But what if the embryo was meant to be a hundred times more powerful, more needed by the Creator? How do you see that?"

"What if Mary had aborted the Christ child… She was warned. But how would any woman know she's carrying a genius? And if she suspects – intuitively senses it – will she be ready to raise him, able to provide for him? What if she's a beggar, starving and barefoot… Can you imagine how many aborted geniuses-diamonds the Earth has lost? How many died in earthquakes, wars, accidents?"

"Well, that's exactly why we exist, dear Chance – to prevent it.

And at the Last Judgment only Loa's computer will know – who was right, and who, bluntly put, sinned: the person, her guardian angel, Chance, or Fate… During the Great Cleansing, all the waste will be destroyed, and the diamonds of various grades will become God – for a strand of God's hair is also God…" chirped radiant, beautiful Fate, as elemental and lovely as nature itself: now snow, now sun, now wind… now rain. A marvelous creature. Milk and blood.

"What's going to happen to Halya, anyway, who – by the way – is well acquainted with our long-standing subject 24-X-315?"

"Are you planning to intervene?"

"No, no… she'll have to climb out on her own. Maybe, somehow, a little diamond will come of her yet."

"I know her fate, of course, but I won't tell you. Revealing who Death will choose next – that's the greatest sin I could commit against the Creator…" Fate removed her white cap and revealed her beautiful poetic hair. "If people knew for certain that all true lovers reunite in heaven, even then their souls would be afraid: what if I end up alone, like in that old joke… And would there be enough partners for everyone? Say what you like, Loa's really spun this all brilliantly – a theoretical perpetual motion machine…"

"You know, Fate," Chance interrupted her in a vast, heavy tone. "I'm tired of this Kali – with its rains and coffee, its beautiful pretension and the inscrutable soul of its stone crosses, the ones all the invaders shot at. Everyone's had a go at Kali. Let's spin up something new."

"Let's!" Fate rang like a bell. "THE CULTIVATING DIAMONDS continues… Oh, how I loathe the fake ones!"

HELLISH PARADISE

After Kali, Fate and Chance naturally longed for something radically, polemically opposite – healthy, unfeigned, rooted in truth. They picked up the traces of 24-X-315 again and followed the thread of Fate...

Roosters crowed in the sunlight; a fat-cheeked cat basked under the defenseless, cloudless sky; the air smelled of fields, natural freedom, and wholesome love. Everything was filled with Spirit, with God; everything was conflictless and somehow wisely calm. A being initiated into spiritual mysteries knew: peace in the Creator's Laboratory, like happiness, is a very relative thing – momentary, stretched out at best...

...Onto the threshold stepped a very old grandmother, scattering wheat for the chickens. Out came a tall old man – the love of her distant youth, who, even at seventy, had cheated on her with some woman from the neighboring village, where he traveled with his dearly cherished black horses, whom he loved the way girls love puppies.

Near the church, a sprightly little Romani boy, quick as dusky mercury, begged an old villager to let him sit on his mare. "If only they could see me now! If only the gypsies saw me now, on a horse!" the boy burst with excitement, buzzing and humming... The villager, his eyes naive yet harsh with life's burdens, wiped away an uninvited tear with a sleeve soaked in silent torment.

Suddenly, a teenage girl ran up to them – also of Romani blood, potentially and fiercely beautiful, like a black rose, lithe and ringing, flexible as the flame of a free Romani steppe fire.

"Give me your little sister and I'll give you the horse!" the old man teased the boy.

A flicker of some deep ancestral doubt flashed across the boy's childlike face, already touched by life's heavy questions...

"No, no," he finally whispered loudly, "I can't... no-no..."

He didn't say that his mother or father would scold or beat him; he didn't make excuses. You could hear that the decision came from his small, natural heart – natural like nature itself: the boy would not trade his sister for a horse...

Such scenes of rural life (far from idyllic, who knows) were observed by Fate and Chance. Time and Space, connected by their electronic – or whatever – link, joined them.

They all decided not to remain passive observers this time, but to exercise their power over the lives of the inhabitants of the Creator's laboratory – or rather, one of His laboratories, called Earth.

By the village tavern, drunks lay sprawled like forget-me-nots.

A man plowed a field.

A barefoot boy herded cattle back from pasture.

Lovers rolled in the hay that smelled of vast stars.

A lonely grandmother clumsily chopped up her dear laying hen beside a crumbling hut.

Her neighbor – an old man of whom the village language and literature teacher once wrote in his highbrow "Diary": "The greatest vileness is the vileness of old men" – was reading a newspaper he had found in his garden. Adjusting his glasses with one cracked lens, he muttered:

"Astrophysicists claim that about fourteen billion years ago, from some kind of dense clump, our Universe was born and immediately began to expand in all directions. This expansion continues. Thus, our Galaxy – the Sun, the myriad stars, the Earth – everything is drifting farther and farther apart. What will happen next, no one knows. Whether this expansion will continue, or finally stop. Then the Universe will begin to contract again…" The old man, Yevtukh, added: "…like a great heart." "This contraction will mark the beginning of the 'end of the world.' But in that case, it won't be soon. After all, the Universe is infinite. Even the nearest galaxy observable with current technology is about 2,5 million light years from Earth. Not only can the human mind not grasp such a distance, it can't even comprehend how far light travels in one minute. And here – millions and billions! (Light travels 300,000 kilometers per second.)"

The old man lit his pipe and looked up at the sky. He suddenly felt an overwhelming desire to go to the village cemetery – to his wife, who had been sleeping the eternal sleep for five years.

To most (nearly all) villagers, Yevtukh seemed harsh, cruel, inhuman, stingy – even godless. But in truth...he had never done deliberate harm to a living creature. He had simply been, for the past twenty years, not quite of this world. And people do not love the otherworldly, the lofty – they burden them with devilish traits, with sorcerers' signs. Grass, after all, does not offer itself to people obtrusively – nor harm them, though they often mistake it for a weed.

So the old man fed his three hens and set off. His cat, as old and as slow as he, but in his own feline way, followed behind.

They came to a cross-winged grave. Sat down. Yevtukh lit his pipe again, pulled out a yellowed newspaper, and began murmuring – not to himself, but as if to his wife, with whom he had lived and endured his whole life, with war, with funerals of loved ones… of his daughter. "There was blood, and there was mother's milk too." His wartime friend Oleksiy – rest his soul – used to say.

"A serious threat to Earth's inhabitants may also come from large asteroids or meteorites colliding with our planet. On March 23, 1989, a large asteroid crossed Earth's orbit at a point where Earth itself had passed just six hours earlier...

Recently, the ozone layer has thinned significantly, and in some places, ozone holes have appeared.

Earthquakes also pose a threat to humankind.

Another enormous danger to the planet's inhabitants are known and unknown diseases. A few centuries ago, the plague and cholera were considered God's punishment. In 1347, the plague wiped out forty million people in Europe.

In 1980, for the first time, a new terrifying and, for now, incurable disease was mentioned – AIDS. How many it will kill – no one knows.

As we see, there are many reasons for the 'end of the world,' and all of them are quite serious. So, humanity is capable of destroying itself…"

The old man lit a match to the yellowed page of the newspaper and sent it off into the wind. Calmly smiling, he took a piece of bread from his pocket, gave some to the cat, some to his wife... and sat there and sat. Sat and sat.

Meanwhile, on the full moon, a light rain began to fall. The air filled sharply with the scent of freshness, budding leaves, and with it, the not-yet-vanished memory of last year's fallen leaves – in short, the past…

Nine-year-old Ostap hid beneath the featherbed, because the power had gone out in the village, and his grandmother had lit a kerosene lamp. It was magical and cosy. The incompleteness of life was made whole by the wild, perhaps even boundless, endless dream-fantasy-fable. After the storytellers, there's no room in the spiritual realm for philosophers, priests, or even pure poets.

And so, Ostap (or 24-X-315 to Loa, Time, Space, Chance, and

Fate) vividly imagined himself, to the point of pain, with a motor on his back like Karlsson-on-the Roof. He was flying through the night forest, living in a warm hollow, helping birds, animals, and grasses: here he bandaged the wing of a stork injured by a poacher – the stork weeping with the gaze of the Universe upon the Universe; here he grafted a broken wild white rose, spoke with her about the wind, the stars, and the seafloor, which he had never seen but could picture vividly – with sunken Atlantises, Greek amphorae, and Roman spirit…

Everything divine took on human shape, every blade of grass grew into itself again, glass came to life. The world seemed vast and tender – though in truth, it was his soul that was that way: gifted, created by the Creator. And it was neither fault nor merit...Neither fault nor merit.

It was neither Ostap's fault nor merit that he wasn't like the other children – that they felt this strongly, always set him apart, wanted to beat him, but for some reason feared him. That they feared him, but also gravitated toward him. That the old village teachers were baffled by his independence and his hunger for books. But life is life: birth, death, injury, holidays, weekdays...the great churn, the swirl, the mystery, the malt, the salt, the grass, the little cloud, God, the devil, blood, dust, moonshine, song...flight.

An eternal flight, like in a dream – that is the only thing truly suited to a Loa soul, to an Artist: a flight, swift and eternal – so that outside the window, a kaleidoscope of faces, flowers, stars, winds, and inside the soul – song and wind, song and wind...Ah!

As a child, Ostap nearly drowned three times, fell off a rooftop onto bricks twice...was caught in a barn fire set by neighbor boys. In short, his heart acutely sensed the game of Chance and Fate. A strong and tender invisible hand led him through life and tempered his soul, GREW THE DIAMOND, hurling him – unseen – into steep curves of trial and pulling him out by a hair from the winged embrace of beautiful (and not-so-beautiful) death.

With his distant cousin and close friend Andrii Veres, he would spend entire summer days at the pond, fishing. One day, the boys noticed that green pond frogs leapt onto a baitless hook, mistaking it for a fly. Andrii teasingly lured a hungry frog – it took the hook. Spinning the poor creature in a circle of five to seven meters, he flung it against an oak. The frog clung to the trunk, slid to the roots – and "croaked".

Ostap Shablii, too, joined in with sporting-hunting excitement. His emotionally deep nature took it so to heart – like everything he did – that he killed probably twice as many naïve creatures as his friend. That night, he felt so wretched in his soul that it turned into physical nausea.

The next day, Andrii resumed the frog games. But some madly earthly-heavenly power, some intuition, FORBADE Ostap from doing it again. It was as if a sheaf of otherworldly light had been thrown at him, and a fresh, sharp wrinkle – like the smile of a strange star – fell between his brows. Though hardly anyone noticed.

Then there was a pigeon killed by accident, a crow shot, a sparrow. Ostap felt such sorrow for all of them. Their lifeless bodies forced him to feel SOMETHING – something dense and primal – and to understand in ways beyond comprehension. That something was a vast ONENESS: everything is part of the soul, the soul is part of God, and so, everything equals God…ape-like humans, god-like people…

Fate kept taking his loved ones away – one after another, one after another… He grew up burying. Chance let him feel and grasp that there is SOMEONE, SOMETHING, to which, to whom we all ultimately come. Space showed him the world in quantitative terms. Time adjusted and apportioned the number of tempering cycles in this or that DIAMOND FURNACE. Loa, probably, only smiled in that grandfatherly way and thought to himself: "What different children there are! Tell one: 'Petryk, don't go there, the old witch Baba Yaga lives there' – and the child is afraid, obeys. Tell another the same thing – he won't believe your word, but he'll go, cautiously, stealthily, and check whether Baba Yaga really lives there. Then he'll believe. There are even some who never believe in Baba Yaga. I don't like those. They're not DIAMONDS. Diamonds are the ones who doubt but still go, believe, feel…'the Spirit of truth, whom the world cannot accept, because it neither sees Him nor knows Him'…"

Reading books and absorbing the world like a sponge, 24-X-315 began to understand and feel that there are vegetarian plants, that nature knows neither mercy nor cruelty, that in 20–30 years AIDS might wipe out half the Earth's population, that "freedom to the free, paradise to the blessed" (is paradise unfreedom, then?), that ancestors somehow help their descendants… that there can be such a beautiful autumn that it becomes entirely self-sufficient (money or love paradoxically turns it into sorrow); that people, as a rule, remember only their grandfather, at best their great-grandfather – beyond that is the edge of memory, and therefore, of pain.

Ostap Shablii nearly broke when trying to comprehend paradoxes like: through good one can commit evil – and vice versa. That is, the matter of false and true values – diamonds. One can believe in God and hate priests – and vice versa… again, the question of genuine versus inflated values.

Billions of books have been written by humankind, billions of aphorisms composed – and yet every second you must err anew, laugh anew, cry anew, fight anew, be born and die anew. And LOVE anew.

In his more mature years, reflecting with his heart on the nature of universal Good and Evil, holiness and sin, Shablii came to the conclusion that "sin is only sin when you believe it is. True LOVE justifies EVERYTHING." And only a diamond-like human heart and the ultra-precise computers of Loa, Space, Time, Fate, and Chance could truly register that authenticity. These five, gathered like young scientists, studied and tempered the diamond code named 24-X-315 – casting him into one high-temperature furnace after another. His body aged, but his SPIRIT hardened, becoming God-like, because it was becoming a particle of God…

Too short was the term allotted to the body of Ostap Shablii in the Earth-laboratory to contain the eternity of Loa's spirit. God is spirit. Humans are carriers of spirit. Therefore they are fragments of God, therefore they are – potential gods. But not all. Only – DIAMONDS. Surely, there must be other laboratories where other varieties of souls are being grown and tempered.

Loa pressed a button, and 24-X-315 appeared on the screen. He stood in the forest, over an anthill. Beside him – his car.

A hunting rifle slung behind his back. He had gone hunting for his own soul, that is, for balance. He didn't want to kill or destroy anything. But he was both primitive and of the distant future. He could have poured a bucket of gasoline over the anthill and hurled a flaming twig of viburnum or fir. He could have stopped this world of ANTS, just as a human can destroy the world of humans – with the push of a button, launching a missile with a nuclear warhead. But all he could truly create was a SONG. And even in that, there was the eternal, drawn-out, aching dissatisfaction.

"So little can be said, expressed!" His inside self-cried.

"Do you know, Ostap, what Darwin said?" His beloved approached him and took his hand, this woman with whom he was, for the first time, far from people who were filling their lives more and more…

"What?"

"Even Darwin said that the idea of a human eye evolving by natural selection seemed absurd in the highest degree, and yet, he believed it was the case."

"The eye… by way of evolution? No. Can't be…"

Ostap lifted her in his arms and carried her into the tall grasses reaching to the starry sky – grasses that sang a song about the essential.

"I don't know whether this is how it really is or not," she said, "but to dream, surely, is no sin."

Fate, Chance, Time, and Space all laughed.

Loa kissed Fate on the forehead – and laughed too.

The Cultivating Diamonds continued.

Time brought up a new fragment on the screen.

II

HUNTERS AND PREY

"That's it. That's it. That's it! *Tabula rasa.* The past – my personal past – is no more. Tomorrow I start from scratch." Taras Kryshtalskyi nearly shouted, hoping as many people as possible would hear him – he'd be ashamed not to keep his word. Like a die-hard smoker swearing off cigarettes. "No titles, no merits, no defeats – not even mistakes anymore..."

He truly needed the meditation, the ritual – to change himself, while the world did not need it, neither the tree-people, nor the people-trees, who stood grieving in equal silence over the graves of their children: cherry trees and women. To change himself so that he might change something, someone. To spark a revolution of explosion or calm, of scattering or gathering stones.

The servant-masters of the universe – Space (the body) and Time (the spirit) – were fiercely and creatively doing their work. They were around Taras, inside him – everywhere, always. When they merged within him, Kryshtalskyi felt happy.

So it was here too, among Siberian fur hunters, the company he found himself in when he visited a flight attendant he'd met during a journalism assignment, back when he headed a section of a religion newspaper.

Her parents – former political prisoners – welcomed this grand-son of fellow political prisoners with simple kindness. The traces of his ancestors had long been swept away by the blue pelts of Norilsk, Transbaikal and Tiksi storms.

Grandfather Ivan advised him on what rifle to buy, boots, coat, hat, gloves.

The fur hunters, these fury chasers, were open, unguarded, natural – therefore strong, like children. They could drink, brawl, and then offer their lives for a friend. They'd repent, then wordlessly go about their work, their eyes full of blackberry sorrow. They told the truth – raw, bitter, painful, and strong.

After the sly yellow gray hustle of the city – the endless chase after...oneself – this freedom of truth and truth of freedom was intoxicating. It felt so good. To wrap oneself in bear and lynx skins, grill great fish over a fragrant fire, brew teas from proud herbs, and – most of all – know the truth: white is black, fire is ice, love is simply: "I want you. Yes? No?"

Earth – fire – breath – water. The primal-Christian bond of the fur hunters, the fury chasers… didn't exclude a different quadrant: vodka – tobacco – woman – beast. They tried not to speak of God. Of children – they spoke with reverence.

The Siberian wilderness quickly stripped away any contrived naivety or masked bravado of worms, cocoons, butterflies. The alphabet of life's joy here truly boiled down to ten commandments, perhaps Christian, whose password, the key, was one word: honesty. Honesty in self-deception and the deception of others – human and animal. Honesty as the soul's openness and the furred closure of the body, which lovers studied – sacred, sinful – like a homeland, like animal tracks…

Snobs and social climbers, preachers and lard-loving patriots didn't last long here. Nor did sly boozers or overly virtuous clean eaters.

To eat dry alcohol or drink raw yeast, sleep beside a goat or similar exotic tricks seemed like child's play for people bored even under death's gaze – that gaze that reminded of the water of taiga swamps, still for millennia.

"Taras, that girl you keep calling – does she love you?" asked the flight attendant.

"Love is a heavenly gift. Mutuality's at the bottom of the list." Taras smiled. "Especially since men often separate sex and what they call love. They can be entirely different things. It's not even a…"

"Betrayal?"

"Something like that."

"What if it's real?" The sky-born Siberian pressed.

"Want the masks off here too?" He lacked the strength for irony.

"I know it hurts. I know people flinch from those like you. They respect them – and fear them. Just like they do geniuses."

"What kind of genius am I, if I'm still not sick of life, haven't stepped over myself in disgust, and if my brain hasn't yet composed something called *The Theory of Relativity* or *The Periodic Table*, *The Origin of Species*, at the very least? What matters is the work – childlike and global."

"So, do you love her?" The flight attendant asked again, nearly pulling back the final veil. "And don't start philosophizing or psycho analyzing – damn you!"

"Yes." The man who had been initiated into true hunters answered without exclamation, preserving deep inside the right to a post-truth ritual: he feared everything, so when it was necessary, he feared nothing. The key was to accept danger as a gesture of Fate – Fate that often worked through Chance in one Space or another.

The young flight attendant almost managed to play indifference. Only the bark mask of a century-old fir tree grew slightly damp with fog.

"And what if I hang myself and leave a note: *'I blame Taras Kryshtalskyi for my death?'*"

"I'll have no choice but to hang myself too – or shoot myself. And future archaeologists, some new Shakespeares, will write that there once were two celestially strange ones...But enough. Time to sleep. I've got to hunt tomorrow – or rather, already today. Hunt the beast."

They blew out the kerosene lamp and curled up together, nervously submitting to nature. Without analysis. With resistance that only sharpened desire.

The harsh, sometimes cruel naivety of the sharply continental wilderness cost many their fingers – or worse. Sometimes the hunter and prey switched roles, and the tiger, looping its fatal tracks, stalked its fiercest enemy – man. In the grand scheme, it was fair. The killer gets killed. The killer suffers more… however you look at it.

The mist, laced with the first rays of sun, lingered gently, kissing the tear-blurred panes. The alarm clock bubbled in panic.

"So, you're really going?" asked the flight attendant, taking Taras by the hand.

"Blood's calling! Awoo!"

"I dreamt of children last night."

"And what will come of it?" asked Kryshtalskyi, dousing himself in cold water, trying to sound detached.

"Trouble…"

"Trouble's in the big cities. Or in stupid, ragged villages. But here – tree-people, people-trees…"

The family sent off their hunter properly. Grandfather fixed the skis for winter hunting. Grandmother prayed. The flight attendant dozed on the still-warm spot of the "fury chaser." Sweet-absurd dreams swirled through the sleepy folds of her brain, spawning surreal visions: a trembling, ringing, nearly youthful couple making love in the March forest. Seed sprayed, ran, smeared across flowers, trees. A year later, when they returned, strange voices sighed around them. Voices of children – flower-people, birch-people, maple-people…Some strange mutation had happened in this radioactive zone. A groan-creak hung in the air where love once bloomed – and there was no cure. Someone would come with an axe.
The fairy tale was becoming real – and vice versa.

The flight attendant was silent all day.

That evening, Kolya Yevtushenko ran in and calmly said: "Your guest – he's there. He stepped on a high-voltage wire."

Tragedy is always banal.

So is how people perceive it – regardless of appearances.

A helpless, seemingly spineless civilization. A touch of pollen to metal, current, to the wild heart of a tree – and that's all… Blue-eyed Time doesn't yearn for that. Nor does Space.

Everyone is a killer. Everything is. Even good: it kills evil.

Mercenary electricians from everywhere tore wings from the trees – trees like butterflies striving for Light, bearing and raising children, composing melodies with the wind for a confused world, hating hysteria, maybe loving revolution – but only if it was their own, not done to them… To the root, to the root. Let the wolves and deer drink the pine sap. Let not people – who lack measure. In place of a sense of oneness with all living things, they have a conscience. So conscientious they don't even need intelligence. They think they alone know how to laugh and make promises. But in the end, it will be the rats who laugh last…

The cleverest of people destroy deliberately – just to search again for truth. So many possibilities. So many temptations, sinful fears, ghosts of consciousness.

…Taras had stepped on a live electric wire, carelessly, raggedly left behind by the workers laying high-voltage lines.

Electricity – like death, the soul, the Creator – was invisible, unrelenting, powerful.

Crushed with grief, the Siberians buried Kryshtalskyi in the hard Earth, not even taking him to church, where there was less gold than in the autumn forest, and a priest had to be paid less green-dollars than grew on spring and summer trees.

The flight attendant touched Taras' forehead with her lips. A jolt passed through her. The mystery between two people has its current too.

She wanted to hide – from everything, even from God. Grief truly does return one to the logical-mystical unity of their primal tribe.

"Nothing dies. Everything just changes." The hunter-philosopher comforted her.

And the local priest added:

"That's how it is. People don't believe, don't believe – and then grief wrings them out, and just like that, they're one of ours!"

Like Aeolus's grandchildren, the thoughts of those who had come to love the otherworldly hunter swirled.

Taras Kryshtalskyi was wisely buried in the earth.

His funeral rite was held by the eschatological hour.

LOA'S RESEARCH CENTER

"You've grown completely insolent, kid!" Chuckled Space, weathered by the last births of supernovae. "Quit your computer games and tricks – time to get to work: cultivating and seeking diamonds for the continuation of Existence. Our latest hopes – seeds – have failed us. Some were lured by anti-Loa money, others by anti-Loa fame. And molding a diamond from dung is a thankless task. An average person… The sum of average people will yield a large average person – plenty of flesh, but little Spirit."

"How about 24-X-315?" Asked the boy-Time, looking up from his Universal Computer.

"I don't want to know. He already belongs to the Old One, not us. Loa tries to claim those like him quickly. We must maintain our natural neutrality."

"So do we wash our hands of it and pick another candidate?"

"If we're hunters…"

"But who are we?" Time rubbed his little hands together.

"Who are we? Regretfully, mutable, like everything. In black holes, Time and Space trade places. And when technically advanced beings finally invent – or rather build – photon engines and start flying, flying… and if they fall into a black hole…"

"They'll diamond-ify instantly?"

"Maybe…"

"Fascinating! Let's help the sentient beings conquer Space sooner!"

"Me?" said Space.

"Why only you?" Time replied quicker… more temporally. The two laughed with free laughter.

They feared neither poverty nor death, nor illness nor unbelief, nor persecution for faith. In other words – they were free. They had a goal, health, relatively good looks, clothing… That sort of thing. None of it was a fault or a merit.

"Well then, we'll seek new diamonds and grow them. Cause a bit of mischief." Said Space.

"We're both killers and healers."

"We're eternal and fleeting."

"We're slackers and sages."

"Marching into Nothingness."

"Only slaves serve us…"

"And the Devil lends a hand…" Time gestured rhythmically in sync with rhyme.

"Made that up yourself?" Winked Space, smoothing his balding head with an habitual motion.

"Impromptu. Yep."

"And why haven't you mentioned Fate? Or Chance?"

"Why not… Haven't got to that yet."

"They're not our servants, obviously…"

"And we're not theirs."

"To be sure. No one serves anyone unless they choose to. Some pray to others, some imitate them."

"Fate and Chance have their own life-being. They're our colleagues, right?"

"Of course. Alright, start the Program."

Time, like a flying pianist, touched the keys with his fingers. From the screen came the scent of a night granary – grain, chaff, old harness. Rats rustled. There were so many that the poor old man, it seemed, had spent his whole life battling them – and never won. Lately, his mind had begun to slip. He would take his axe and head to the forest – to chop wood, even though his whole yard was already piled with it.

"Listen, Time, he clearly doesn't perceive you adequately."

"So his yard is filled with me? Am I a pine tree, a fir, an aspen?"

"No, of course not – that's all me: sea, stars, wind!...Though they do say 'winds of time'...I only account for that!"

"Let's not divide responsibilities too seriously. Let's treat it as a game."

"You mean to say you don't see Existence as one big Game? Maybe it's time we got off these Computers and stretched our bones?"

"You mean jump into a black hole? You want pain?"

"Uh-huh. Something like that."

"But first let's finish watching this fragment."

And so they watched.

The old man returned from the forest, muttering prayers. Quarreled with his old woman who ran the household. He had taken all the icons off the walls and hid them from her at their neighbors – to keep them "from being sold," or so he thought. Lately he'd developed a strange affection for a big-headed, tubby cat named Boomba. He fed only Boomba and never kicked him out of the house. "That cat's gotten cocky." The old woman muttered. Boomba ignored the rats. He ignored the old woman too. He felt protected. His cheeks puffed more and more, his nose grew soft.

Time accidentally hit another key. On the screen appeared Taras

Kryshtalskyi, buried in the earth.

"Oh, look!" cried Time. "That's the old man's relative."

"All people, all living beings – are relatives, kin." Said Space with a touch of skepticism.

IN THE GRAVE

"Op-la!" groaned Kryshtalskyi, rubbing his crusted eyelids in a gesture so habitual it bordered on nausea. "Some madman's delirium...Felt like I'd eaten too much meat with mushrooms and washed it down with milk. Why is it so stuffy? Damn..."

He tried to stretch – hit his head on something hard. Rolled left and right – walls. Sleepiness vanished as if cut by a sickle...Nerves flared. His body, like evening soil, was covered in a salty dew – perhaps vodka, honest and therefore holy.

"What's torturing me like this?" thought Taras. "Probably my conscience. But why would a clean conscience torture me?" In order for one's conscience to be clean, one must use it less… He tried to laugh, but it hurt to laugh. Sores of the soul.

He counted how many women he'd had… Still didn't have control over himself… over the power of idle spirit.

He jerked again. Felt as though he were in a pipe, or a womb – on the verge of being born. Born from the womb… of the Earth.

"I'm in a coffin!" Kryshtalskyi nearly choked on the thought – not a cry, more like he had already died, disconnected.

The irony of it was that he couldn't even manage suicide, to avoid prolonged suffering.

Time stopped, but thoughts scattered faster than photons, faster than the speed of thought itself, darting chaotically like a kaleidoscope of puns and dream-snippets.

The soul was suffocating – more than the body. It was the soul that felt the weight.

At lightning speed, his brain flashed through the most vital images of Tara's life: the sticky, earthy warmth of a mother's body, the first betrayal by the world, the cold loneliness, the face of a light-haired, brown-eyed girl, almost still a child; his grandmother in her coffin; a meadow; a sunlit forest clearing where light air-like flowers bowed to the trees.

Bursts of memory again – retrospective: a cradle, a stork's wing, the bottom of some vast body of water – misty. Not the happiest memories, nor the most painful – just random, disordered. As though a person had grown used to both joy and sorrow, to habit itself, yet remained capable of flight – though only with a long run-up, or maybe just for the run-ups sake. It didn't matter. As long as the soul longed for something.

"Breathe less." A thought pecked at him. "No point in screaming – but maybe just now and then…" He shouted "Help!" and pictured the face of someone walking past his grave. Smiled with his whole heart.

He remembered Gogol, allegedly found flipped in his coffin, and other tabloid horror tales. He thought of people he respected, people he had learned from: again the grandfather, grandmother, his teacher Yevhen Kyrylovych, another schoolteacher… Shelley, Takuboku, Cervantes, Blok, Franko, Bulgakov, Yesenin, Lesya Ukrainka, Nietzsche, Hemingway, Hugo, Goethe, Mercury, Byron, Beethoven, Shevchenko… Their spirits called to him. Fear itself began to feel like joy. The flow of consciousness, of existence, coiled within his skull, lowering damp tendrils…

The instances of personality – Ego, Super-Ego, Id – merged in this Waiting into a single whole, anticipating a black-hole transformation.

Horses in masks, butterfly maidens, grotesque bats from parallel worlds… scents, colours, sounds – and "don't waste your strength, cousin, just sink to the bottom."

Temperature waves would suddenly seize Tara's being, then let go – like a horse to water – and he'd resume counting women he'd "had." There were as many as apples.

He imagined himself as a child in the womb of Mother Earth. The umbilical cord was made of these flashing, fragmentary memories. Pity you could only be reborn with your soul – if such a thing even existed. For even now, belief wrestled with irony, sarcasm, cynicism, and the Great Void.

It wasn't any easier to deceive himself in a living grave.

He shouted again. Everything seemed so simple and familiar: a one-eyed dog on a city street, a hen brooding eggs, golden leaves flying upward, water flowing downward.

He wanted to sob, like a prayer.

He whispered to himself what he knew: "Still, I had too few women. Either they were too beautiful – not their fault – or too ordinary. That too was sacred. And I was lazy. And that was a mistake. I was afraid. And fear – that's a sin." He caught himself thinking, "I've grown used to this kind of life." And smiled naturally.

The lack of air was becoming real.

He imagined himself as a skeleton. Above him – an aspen. Why an aspen? Shivering, sensitive, the last one – both young and ancient.

The urge to cry clenched his throat. Something – probably what people call a conscience – was doing its work. He felt a wild, wolf-like sorrow for children – from dew to stars.

"When will I be born? How much longer? Time passes nothing like we imagine – as if it's swapped places with space in the black holes of our minds." Kryshtalskyi turned his face to the planet's core.

He thought he heard crows above. Crows, definitely. A deep, earthen cleansing was beginning to swell. Only now did the question come: "Why did they bury me?" He recalled going out with a rifle on his shoulder, eating some kind of star like summer berry. Something struck – then sweetness. Damn...

Everything became absurdly clear. No mysticism. But the essential Truth remained hidden… since always. Damn it all.

He cried out long and bright: "I'm a-li-ive!"

More fragments flowed across his inner screen: peasants carrying grain to the barn, forest, the smell of mushrooms, milky strands of another Indian summer, the cat Boomba, murmuring, "scratching his belly," spilled old wine in a long-abandoned village house, emptiness – and a spring meadow. It wasn't yet autumn, but he already longed for spring. The soul's mill endlessly grinding the flour of sorrow. Cursed suffering, cursed aging of loved ones! A piercing nostalgia for nostalgia itself… in struggle – for peace, in peace – for struggle. And round and round it goes. Even wise Earth circles the Sun.

Thoughts, like navel-less but beloved children, buzzed without anchoring. Needed by no one. Unmaterialized.

Salons, white gloves, otherworldly music, foreign wines, relations between people, beasts, molecules, stars – honest and simple as moonshine. Gulls wail, village grandfathers and aged scholars weep.

Cossacks with pipes sat in his soul at oak tables. He wanted to smoke – as a final wish before the edge of eternity. Strangely, in his pocket he found a lighter, plastic, violet, and a pack of American cigarettes. The thought of smoking in a grave made him chuckle. But...if only he had a couple hundred grams of vodka to go with it! Just once...People die from disease, from earthly and celestial catastrophes, from beasts – and most of all, from each other. Diseases come from the micro-world, all else from the macro.

Fear gripped him in hexameter – wave by wave. Strangely, he still had air. Whether that was good or bad, he didn't know. Better to die of hunger, or suffocation?

And again, like dark-browed water, flared memory-thoughts, fantasy-thoughts, analytical impressions. Colours, sounds, smells. Sweet pains and painful pleasures. Haymaking, school friends – Yasha, Kostya, Mila, Bohdan...Some were already gone… Vitya Morhayenko had drowned. Leska had twelve kids.

Etched from a tight, creaking moonbeam, the image of Ruslana appeared. It was sacred. It healed, like a plantain leaf. He kissed the earth. Lightly. As though one half had finally found its other.

His heart ticked slowly, like a wind-up alarm clock.

Taras Kryshtalskyi screamed again – wildly.

Above (or maybe below?) cranes began to cry. Earthly-earthly. Celestial-celestial.

A primeval scent of blackberry blood – or Dnipro water – slid into his throat.

And then, from above, something laughed.

A jolt of electricity surged through Kryshtalskyi's dampened veins.

CHANCE AND FATE

A fated chance, a chance-shaped fate – like God's pseudonyms. It could be that way.

Chance and Fate cannot have children. Like iron, they don't even need gestures, expressions like love and hate, non-functional, naturalistic or psychological-philosophical categories.

There is no destruction without construction – and vice versa.

Chance loved Fate. He subtly felt the reciprocity. They would part ways and reunite again, drinking wine with the romantic name "Milk of a Beloved Woman"...ilk of a loved omen...but, it never went further than that.

By the logic of atom-universe construction, they had no right to have children?

Who would those children be?.. Angels? Demons? Demiurges?

Perhaps all spirits are "illegitimate," extra-divine children of Chance and Fate, of Time and Space – or spirits are the result of cross-breeding between Chance, Fate, Time, and Space and mortals: the noble and the low, the different?

No one knows. Everyone lives. Beautifully and sadly.

They cultivate Time, and Time, in turn, cultivates personalities.

Personalities (diamonds), "are not afraid to be just; they are philosophers unafraid to be kind; poets aspiring to be humane." So said Olivier Perrin.

"Oh you, Fate, what have you done?" – as the song goes – said Chance.

"Don't sing too early in the morning, it's time to get to work." Croaked Fate like an average banal housewife.

"What, wrap another scarf around Isadora Duncan's wheel? Send Soshenko to Shevchenko in the Summer Garden? Princess Diana? Mother Teresa? Oh please – you decided so! Then why don't you go to hell, woman?!"

Fate smiled like a woman. It wasn't the first time – whims... The eternal struggle.

"I give you full freedom, lad." She muttered drowsily, half-dramatically. "I'll manage without you. Still, every one of your actions automatically resolves my problems – though occasionally it mixes the cards. I've long lived by the rule: there is no evil without good."

"Oh yeah. It's great with you, and without you it's even –"

"Worse..." giggled the girl, thin as a stream of honey.

The "sweet couple" swayed back and forth. Both pretended to be offended. But lovers' quarrels...

Maybe they were simply saddened by autumn on their heroes'

Earth. Or maybe it was the plan all along.

You have to drink the chalice to the bottom, to make sure it's not bottomless.

They didn't even remember whether they had sent the bullet into Lermontov – or simply hadn't intervened in his fate.

From the screen cried the canonized of all churches, sects, teachers, priests, saints: possessed young women, mist-bearded elders, whores and philosophers, harpies and true nuns.

The diversity of being in all its manifestations was staggering and calming.

"I know everything, but understand nothing." Sighed those who pondered life while sipping wine from their own skulls.

Neither did Chance and Fate understand the world completely – nor did Time and Space.

The main laws of dialectics were not a cage-diagram for the truth-bird, but a seed in its light little belly.

And the Mill turned.

Who's the wind in it? Who's the stone? Who's the grain? Who's the flour? Each must decide for themselves.

And what's the point in philosophizing idly if even Arthur Schopenhauer "gained nothing from his philosophy, though it took much from him."

As for psychology, they say it's all quite simple: to unlock a person, love them.

And don't strive for eternal life – just try to drink your fill from this one.

These words, attributed to Pindar, are truly among the wisest of global spiritual testament.

And the rest – Marxist believers, inquisitor-priests, Spartacus wanting to seize power from patricians and hand it to the plebs, ravens flying in a key – are just constants.

Interesting to know, useful to remember, so it's not boring in the repetition...

"You never think about our children!" Said Chance suddenly, overcoming himself – "Our spiritual offspring – geniuses."

"Good thing they were always taken care of (like grandchildren) by the elders – Space and Time." Replied Fate, closing the door with banal finality.

"That bitch!" Time spat after her. "So you want to invent mythology? Spawn all kinds of swamp spirits? Tie yourself up with unclean things? You just wait! Renewal's coming! Time is a boy again. And soon the Creator will make you a girl too. Don't overstep! Don't be too cocky."

The blissful storm between Chance and Fate really did affect the lives of beings, sometimes sharply redirecting or even erasing their awkward and at times deeply artistic biographies.

Fate knew how to hide passion behind aloofness, sin behind bliss, pain behind a smile.

The cosmic night between Fate and Chance lasted as long as had long ago been programmed by the Creator.

At last they bitterly longed for one another again.

They remembered the unbearable things – the tender touches, frost-spark glances, red foaming wine in thin, tall glasses, the "unsayable, blue, tender."

Pure, sacred, searingly unbearable, sinfully beautiful was the desire to meet the one who seemed so real, so truly your other half, your very self, the Universe, everything – salty, bitter, honeyed, mortal and heroic.

Chance dared to call her.

"You love your enemies?" Fate asked, coquettishly, almost mockingly.

"You're not my enemy..." Chance blurted out without thinking.

"So you don't love me?! So I'm no one to you?.."

"I love you!" He shouted, feeling how long that word had twisted in the depths of his harmonies-discords, constructions-destructions. Relief.

"You're my enemy, enemy, enemy! If you like..."

"Ah, so you want power over me?!"

"I want power over myself..."

"But I'm your other half."

Chance felt good – almost too good, to the point of nausea, because the body cannot bear moments of such soul-crushing happiness.

"Everyone wants power." Fate continued. "Those who don't have enough scream into the Cosmos, waiting for echoes."

"So love is also power?"

"The subconscious desire for it."

"You're getting too clever."

"A little wit never hurt nobody."

"No matter how smart we are, we can't hide from God."

"And He from us?"

"Especially from women...Strange how the 'main' gods were always given male names: Perun, Allah...the Son of God, Christ."

"Maybe so women would love them more. Did you notice how they cling to Christ? How they lick Him clean!" the girl improvised theatrically.

"There's probably something to that. Churches really are filled with more women than men.

Especially the border-crossers – the ones already preparing for what lies beyond..."

Fate and Chance met eyes. He timidly took her by the finger.

The golden October of Earth was theirs. The evening turned violet.

They were one again. And spoke of their shared purpose.

THE GRAVE

"Come on, Kalenyk, dig. Right here. This damned Siberian soil doesn't just drain electricity from a body – it'll suck out your soul, your spinal cord." Said Uncle Mikhal to his older colleague – another gravedigger, just like him.

"Yeah. It's damp." The other replied tersely. "Just let's hope he doesn't fall into a lottery dream."

"Lethargic sleep..."

"Ah. And if his soul returns to his body – well, there's no chance of that. He was a strong man."

Kryshtalskyi's misty dream-state was completely gone. He screamed again. Louder, louder… not even sure if anyone but the One he'd begun to believe in – out of fear – could hear him.

The gravediggers, emotionally preoccupied with themselves, heard nothing.

"Hey, old man," Kalenyk said dryly, "you sure we're not digging him up too early?"

"Maybe. I'll go grab a bottle. Can't figure this out sober. As they say: Either ditch the cross or zip up – can't have it both ways."

"Let's go together."

Kryshtalskyi heard a faint clink above him: someone – like a Shakespearean character – was brushing earth off a shovel onto stone or metal. Then silence.

Unmourned, a vast Emptiness pressed down on Taras again. It got even worse. Just like always, after hope had been murdered.

For the first time, he felt he lacked oxygen.

The wait for a miracle dragged on.

A deep human hatred – toward his Fate, or maybe Chance, or finally just himself – punched him in the chest.

"In this world, every gesture – every motion, mystical or mundane – is either constructive or destructive. Neutrality doesn't exist," confirmed the hunter buried in Siberia. "You're either growing or degrading. How long you remain in dead space depends on your social and emotional temperature."

His ordered thoughts began to scatter, more and more. Taras' mental ECG would've looked like a village fence after a wedding, and his weary body – like the pillows in a hospitable peasant home.

He was ready – philosophically, yogically – to dissolve into molecules. He remembered the line from a song: "Don't let me recognize the first instant of the end."

Kalenyk and his friend ran into a poetess whose mother they'd buried just days ago. She began pouring her grief into their glasses. The vodka had pepper in it. Strong stuff. Only a sick atheist could've refused. They drank with soul.

Only real priests, poets, and deep gravediggers could drink like that – earthly, with talent, without speeches or toasts, pitying lions in cages, never offending people or killing flies – because those, too, are Universes. Because you can't make them, only destroy them... and that's far too easy.

Golden autumn, golden sun, golden bliss wrapped around them like cocoons. Like a divine equilibrium for a larva – not quite a caterpillar, not yet a butterfly. And it felt good. It didn't know its future. Nor did those around it. They didn't understand why it was already pecking outward with its still-infantile, yet promising, wings. "Nonsense, absurd!" whispered the petty crowd. But it's neither the butterfly's fault nor its merit that it left the cosy cocoon.

"Hey, old man," Kalenyk hiccuped, "you remember what we're supposed to be doing?"

The "old man" nodded, grabbed his head like it was a globe. His two index fingers landed on "Italy" and "Japan."

Physically, they could no longer walk. Though their thoughts diffused. Photons could not keep up with them.

Kryshtalskyi somehow knew all this from inside the grave. He imagined who would cry for him, and how. "Let it be fewer people – but more sincere." Alongside despair came a faith in some higher justice: things really were the way they were supposed to be...

He felt that his body and his I – his Self – were becoming separate. His heart and brain kept looping through sacred-sinful, sinful-sacred thoughts, landing on this conclusion: "I subconsciously tormented women – bringing them to desire, then leaving them at the very moment they were ready for the union of plus and minus, male and female essence…" His desires split, sharply, into simple and complex: to eat, to sleep, to make love – versus glory, wealth, power… "praise from men," which "robs us of praise from God."

His body, meanwhile – pure physical matter – did what it would. Its energy likely came from some other source. It was compressing like a black hole, preparing for one final, desperate leap – from cocoon into larva or butterfly.

Neither guilt nor merit.

Not yet reflexive convulsions, not yet action.

Taras Kryshtalskyi lunged up, strained every salted fiber of muscle – and rose to his knees. That kneeling gave him more hope than wings ever could have. He howled like a beast. Again, again, and again he strained. His pupils narrowed. In them, the Sun cried – though his face was covered in dirt. No – it was the Moon. A full Moon.

Kryshtalskyi stood on solid ground.

The grave had turned out not to be deep at all!

The fear of freedom struck him again – reminding him that he existed. But this was a different freedom now. Local. Understandable. Not that otherworldly one he'd grown so philosophically and psychologically attached to – and couldn't bear. He'd tried to escape to that other freedom like to a mother. As if two hands shaking –

could both resist and embrace one another at once.

"Well, goddamn…" was all Taras could say, feeling, truly and deeply, the futility of the Word, regardless of whether it was in the beginning or in the end.

He remembered that, according to American scientists, when the Moon is overhead, things weigh a gram less. "Well, that's something," he thought. "All our virtues are just victories over fear of the unknown."

He laughed unnaturally – not smiled, but laughed. And that forced laughter turned into something real – just as a physical movement of the lips can stir the soul. Not only the other way around. "We gather stones not our own, scatter fruits we never grew," came a line from one of his own poems.

Grabbing onto the cross like a drunk clutches a friend, Taras resembled a character from Gogol or Bulgakov.

The gravediggers were taken away by the police, who happened to be helping the state security service intercept some international drug mafia bosses rumored to be having a picnic nearby.

Arrogant, tuxedoed agents smirked with meaning, as if scorning fate and fearing chance.

And since Kalenyk had grabbed one of them by the chest – defending a "girl" who turned out to be his sister – the agent, almost disguised as a poet, made a signal to the cops. And in the shadow of that gesture, which took on a mystical weight, the gravediggers vanished – sobered by batons and pantomiming the fatalism of their situation.

Since sobriety comes unnaturally fast after a rubber club, a curious, professional major and two sergeants marched them toward a spot – coincidentally near the cemetery – to dog out "the man."

Taking this as drunken confession from cutthroats (what the drunk says, the sober thinks), the agents began tickling their egos in that special, professional way.

The major kicked Kalenyk's friend. Kalenyk responded:

"What d'you want? He's sinless, is he?"

"Ha-ha-hoo!" laughed the major. "Only saints are sinless. But you'll find the money when the gallows grins at you. If not you – your kin."

"That cocoon and caterpillar thing – you nailed it." Said one of the sergeants.

"Yeah. The time comes when we must either expand the cocoon or trim the wings – or else it's freedom… and the price is the fear of death."

"Uh-huh. And you pay for space with time." Muttered the grave-digger who was walking just behind Kalenyk, wincing from a scar on a drunken tear that slipped down.

"Come on, come on, you monsters!" barked the major, jabbing the younger one. "Voluntary confession. Show us where, so to speak…the bodies are buried."

"Y-you see… he should be alive. It was – um – electricity… zapped him." Kalenyk tried to explain with words and gestures.

"Ahh… on the electric chair…" smirked the second sergeant.

The closer they got to the place where Taras Kryshtalskyi had been buried, the faster and harder the gravediggers' hearts pounded. As if they really were returning to the scene of a crime, not to the site of their sacred labor.

Something secret and heavy caught in their throats: they might've "drunk away" the resurrection of Kryshtalskyi – and he could've suffocated...

There they were – the crosses, the grey chapel. Opposite the third row.

LOA'S DIARY

"As long as you keep silent – you pass for a philosopher. True enough. But silence doesn't mean speech. Whether pre- or post-Babel. Silence means sleep – without snoring. Speech means action, killing. Truth is the adequacy of thought to being. One must unite the logical and the magical poles of existence. For that – a thinking, creative matter is needed – though 'don't touch music with your hands' and 'only sound can separate from the body.' Energy. Spirit. A young-eyed old man… Thinking beings, protein-based beings, imagine me in every way possible – and I… am love, homeland, vodka, in short, deception, deception, deception, a narcotic. Whoever IS, deceives – either himself or someone or something –

anything but death, anything but the spermatozoon. The sperm is cunning and insolent, like Me, like Loa. Stubborn. Strong. But without the egg, he is nothing, even if sperm is full of gold. Everyone's an actor. Everything's a performance. The mad pretend to be sane – and vice versa. But whatever the case… to comprehend creation, one must first love it. Oh, even the wisest of beings won't manage to translate me into their language. The most brilliant won't understand – though they may sense Me subconsciously. Let it be as it is, for now. Even Space and Time, Fate and Chance do not understand Me completely – as a part cannot comprehend the whole."

This is roughly how the computer translated Loa's chain of associations: signs, symbols, images. Prearranged deception. Ritual. And the Creator – is Truth.

The translations always came out too human. Reading them was like watching grass grow or talking to a machine. Like it or not, sometimes one thinks: "If 'poetry must be a little silly' (Pushkin), then what bliss it must be to be deliberately silly and devout, simple – and transparent! For some – the bliss of stillness, for others – the bliss of Motion."

COMPUTER CENTER

Time and Space felt themselves trapped in the black hole of consciousness, where, as it's known, they exchanged places: Time moved in circles, Space in a straight line. Alone, like a bullet still in flight. Time grew tired of being a boy and took the shape of a silver-haired philosopher. It felt natural, and therefore comfortable, even moving – because surely, Time and Space have their own Fates, too. It all depends on Chance. Whether they like it or not, they must love those wise, loving dictators. Everyone must. Even Death, as the materialized image of imagination. At the very least, she moves through Space in order to carry out her work: freeing up Time for Space, for Existence. Because nothing and nowhere can exist all at once.

Neither Time nor Space lived for themselves, and so, in sudden fits of despair, their hands would instinctively fall on the computer keys: searching for images, searching for Fate, for diamonds, to help polish them.

Look, old man, how clearly the language of grass, stars, and monastery water is reading from the brain of that oddball – let's call him 24-Y-315, – said Space with a dawn-soft, homey-pie kind of cheer.

Oh, a musical, soulful frame! Looks like the 24-X-315 gene has mutated under the influence of radiation and civilization. Even gods, to be resurrected, must first die… So what do we have here? – Time, bald and plump, leaned over his colleague, looking focused and concentrated.

24-Y-315 – a mutation of 24-X-315! Fascinating. Here, the cat Boomba is speaking with a birch tree into which Uncle Pylyp embedded an axe. The birch weeps silently – about everything. The cat maintains natural neutrality. He's thinking about food. Sniffs out, hears a baby mouse. Eats it. Another, a third. From under an old stump, a mother mouse rushes straight at the cat – to distract him. The baby mouse hides in the golden leaves. A large, true mother, saving her little fool as best as she can, complicates her life to the limit, to that threshold beyond which lies Something. You see – said Space – she was happy. She had become a mother...I was just thinking recently that the greatest misfortune for a creature is to want children but not to be able to Mother. What a void! No wine, no heavens, no erotic fantasies can erase it, can't drown it out – at best, they leave a bitter aftertaste. And living beings fear that void the way soldiers fear tenderness...

Oh, and the mouse was eaten by the usurper cat.

Why "usurper"?

Just for the rhyme: soldier – usurper.

But why didn't 24-Y-315 pull the axe out of the tree? Doesn't he feel the birch's pain? Space asked.

Then the bleeding would only get worse. A paradox, but...the cranes are crying for the homeland. This language of all living things isn't even language any more, it's the hum of sweet, airborne pain. A cry not of ego, but of Conscience fused with instinct.

Humans have been deciphering the language of animals, beasts, plants, and birds since long, long ago – even in caves, falling asleep to the fleshy music of violet fire. They fantasized – and stumbled onto truths they never saw or knew.

Because truth is one, and at the same time, everyone has their own version of it.

Yeah. The truth of an aborted fetus, of its mother, of its father, of Loa...

Yet the law of conservation of energy always prevails: souls do the conscientious work...especially mothers, because the fetus has done nothing wrong to anyone. Except, of course, taken some energy, some health from its mother.

* * *

Galaxies and atoms died-exploded and were born-exploded in the world. Everything pulsed, groaned, radiated, fought with itself and with everything else. Somewhere, ungodly temples grew, drunk preachers wandered among souls, chanting: "Drink the wine – my blood"… Empires crumbled, new ones gathered. Polytheism morphed into monotheism – and then back to polytheism again, only in a different dimension, on a new scale: Perun, Veles, Stribog, Dazhbog… Christ. Christ, Allah, Buddha…? Someday, surely, a united humanity will invent and sculpt One God out of all of them. And then (by the same logic) we'll meet intelligent brothers from other worlds, with their own gods – and again there will be many. And so it will be… up to the limit. If Space is infinite. If Time is infinite. If they're real, concrete. If they're not ruled over by Fate, by Chance, by All, by Everything.

Humanity becomes a god (or an evil demon?) for its younger siblings. And some higher species – gods to us. And in the end – we un-der-stand nothing.

We can only imagine that we do not age, that parallel worlds exist, that souls are immortal. Deification. Self-making. The bankruptcy of Christianity.

Some trust Fate more, others – Chance. Still others – Space and Time. But it's hardest to become a wise, intelligent deadpan… Because "That Power I serve which wills forever evil yet does forever good" – (words of Mephistopheles himself). AND IN THAT LIES THE OPTIMISM OF HUMANKIND.

If you dig too deep, everything gets boring in the end... for people, – yawned Time.

Some could hear how he was, Time: when the sand flows in an hourglass.

Right, let's bring it back to specifics. Let's return to our muttons, – said Space with his usual restrained, subtle smile.

You mean, listen to the conversation of molecules?

Sift through shit… or rather, sculpt diamonds from it.

To learn from humans, from everything. To offer something back. For example, great writers, their words about creators: "The artist's goal is not to provide definitive answers, but to make us love life in all its infinite forms" (Tolstoy). "The artist is a wretched person in whose heart lies hidden suffering, but whose lips are shaped in such a way that when a groan escapes, it becomes beautiful music" (Kierkegaard). "The work of great artists is always a magnificent garden – with both flowers and weeds – not a well-groomed park with neat pathways" (Blok). "Rage and passion – these I consider to be the essential virtues of a writer, the forces that make him write seriously" (Heine).

Time sat down at his computer:

Here's the table: "Distribution of Genius in Space and Time on Planet Earth, Solar System." This is what the computer gave me.

On screen it read: "One potential genius is born per 250 people (i.e. 4,000 per million). Another estimate: 6 geniuses per million. Temporal distribution of geniuses: Before Common Era – 65; CE: 1st century – 13, 2nd – 8, 3rd – 8, 4th – 10, 5th – 4, 6th – 4, 8th–10th – 4, 11th – 3, 12th – 9, 13th – 13, 14th – 22, 15th – 66, 16th – 113, 17th – 106, 18th – 258, 19th – 290. And more quotes: 'A genius shackled to a bureaucrat's desk must either die or go mad' (Lermontov); 'Geniuses are often infantile, lost and unhappy people'…"

As for the most productive decades in the lives of geniuses, the computer revealed: "Ages 20–30 – the bronze decade, 30–40 – golden, 40–50 – silver, 50–60 – iron, 60–70 – tin, after 70 – wooden. The peak comes at 35–40. Average lifespan of a genius: 65.3 years. Those who live longest: historians, lawyers, philosophers, clergy, statesmen. Shortest-lived: playwrights, actors, composers, and poets."

Geniuses always strive to Be. They are characterized by reverse

logic: the ability to retrace chains of reasoning backward, low iner-
tia, mental conciseness and precision, the ability to find non-standard
solutions – and simultaneously, a vagueness of thought, a tenden-
cy to leap from a concrete situation to a "compressed" formula or
symbolic image, to think quickly without suppressing subconscious,
intuitive insight.

"All theory, my friend, dry – but the tree of life" Muttered
Space, turning off the computer just as Fate entered. A blonde. In a
denim suit, red high heels, and a rollneck sweater as dark as night.
Charming – enough to drive you mad. Tender-proud, stubbornly
yielding, alluring and untouchable – she couldn't help but attract.
She both pulled you in and frightened you, with her purity and her
seeming sinfulness; her cosmic earthliness; her earthy cosmicity.

Hello, good afternoon, she greeted them modestly.

O-o-oh! The old men groaned.

What are you up to here?

Listening to grass… Space smiled.

To flies, Time grimaced. Everything is perfect and
immortal in general, but every organism in particular… It takes
just a scrap of metal in an organic heart to stop it.

Exactly what we're fighting for. To create an immortal
organic being, flawless – like Loa. Just. To help a new God come
into being. More precisely – to help him be born: so that his body
is untouchable by fire, water, acid, time, or space, and so that the
spiritual being plays with Fate and Chance, as a child does with
Truth, for Truth, too, is a child: screams and screams – and no one
knows what it wants. Truth has no possessions, only a future and
itself, Space almost meditated. It's easier for a fool to pretend
to be wise than the other way around.

He was tired of transparent logic, of conciseness. He wanted to
be drunk on himself, on diversity, on unity through the struggle of
opposites.

"Take the best from every creature, the most vital," said
Time."Don't muddy the waters, old man. Everything was already
clear, and now you stir it all up again. Have some shame, the girl's
here."

"Every time I drop in, you're philosophizing," chimed Fate.

"Well, in your day, we too!... choked one of the "old farts."

"And it didn't break you?" Teased the second.

"What doesn't break me, makes me stronger." Time quipped.

"Let's just have some wine." Said Space, producing delicate garnet-coloured goblets.

"What are we drinking to?" Fate smiled sadly.

"Well...to lads...or lasses." Space drawled.

"What do you mean 'ol' asses'?" Time nearly shouted.

" Whose asses?" Fate blushed.

"I said 'to lads or lasses'..." Space caught up mid-pour.

"It came out a pun… nice." Concluded Time.

The group burst into laughter. It was genuine. Free of self-consciousness.

The computer screen was showing falling stars.

"Old man, find us a village. A farmer. Someone self-sufficient and simple. Someone not drawn to the other world, untouched by desire. There," said Fate, as if stepping back from a precipice. "I'm tired of loving the chaos."

Space tapped the keyboard.

Roosters crowed. The last crane snapped with its wing the lone thread of "Indian summer," perhaps once woven by the Moirai.

It smelled of hay and dung – horse, cow, straw. There was a desire to fly or to plough the earth. To tickle it. To love it. Gold lay scattered, beautiful, everyone's – and therefore, no one's. Everything was sculpted in dimension. Over millennia. By a thousand ploughs. It was clear – and beautiful. Cursed perfection. Nausea, caused by pain and emptiness, sanctity and sin, sobriety and intoxication. By firewater and underwater flames.

To fly and self-complete – or bury oneself in the earth, and… fly again. Or not be. To believe. In anything. Just to believe. To love. Anyone. To hope. Just to...

Everybody and every soul. All of us.

We divide and conquer. Even gods.

We smell of apples and medicine. Sweet-salty. Like blood. Like organic life itself. Like poems written after the third glass...Like a lover's kiss. Real. Mutual. Heartbreaking.

Fate knew how to make a house a sanctuary.

Two sanctuaries – on screen and in the room – created a bliss in which, like at the bottom of a spring, drama was born. Just as it was meant to be.

Molecules diffuse. Galaxies. Clusters. All eating, reproducing, expanding. Wanting. Longing. And it's good. There is no end. Only play, self-delusion can protect the sensitive substance from premature non being.

Fate, Space, and Time lit cigarettes. Fate – clumsily, dreamily. Doing nothing felt like the highest bliss.

And still. Where is our 24-Y-315? Asked Time, an effective manager, tapping a key.

A cemetery lit up. Nearby – an old prison burial ground.

The team got to work: cultivating a specific diamond, using old recipes.

Then the phone rang. It was Chance, offended.

24-Y-315. RESURRECTION

The gravediggers, accompanied by the police, approached their shovels. Nearly sober now from the wind and stress.

"So? Where's your corpse, huh?" the major smirked, rubbing the corner of his mouth with a thick finger.

Kalenyk's face turned pale. A stubborn, delicate thread of Indian summer clung to his eyelashes. Calm. Irritating.

"Oh, oh! Look! The pit's empty!" Kalenyk's friend gasped. "Come see, where he was. He's gone…"

The major and his sergeants stood there, speechless.

"Earth, take me back to your womb!" Kalenyk cried, suddenly clear-headed. His eyes widened – sunflower-huge.

There was a scent of church for some reason. The hoarse light of the daytime Moon hypnotized, cocooning the soul in a not-from-here-ness, salty as blood warmed over a smoldering fire.

"Well, damn your logic!" the major burst out. "Born – lived – died – that makes sense. But resurrection? That's outside logic."

One of the sergeants fell silent, seemingly for good. The other crossed himself.

"Between inhale and exhale, we're free. Otherwise…"

The major shoved the gravediggers in the back, meaning: "Go. Do what you want."

But no one moved. They clustered together, hesitating.

Kalenyk's friend was the first to snap to:

"Guys, let's follow the trail – or whatever – and go spread the word…"

"Around the world?.." the major smirked.

"The apostles…" Kalenyk revealed a half-drunk bottle from under his coat. Suddenly his boozy-puffed face lit up like a May rose. "Guys, why are you so spooked? Everything's real! The client is done marinating… I told you he got zapped. We buried him, tipsy. And he soared up like an eagle. Broke free, and there you go!" The gravedigger concluded. "And then he went off to the taiga to be with his sweetheart, the stewardess. To love in nature… She's got quite the figure, wears clingy pants, ah! Smells like pine and eternal young fire."

"Yeah, yeah, yeah." Nodded the major.

"Some fear living, so they never die. Others fear dying, so they never live. But that guy, clearly he was aiming to be a personality," added Kalenyk.

Everyone, including the silent sergeant, took a swig straight from the bottle – and followed Kalenyk to the stewardess.

"You know, the dead always stick in my mind by their noses pointing up – if you're looking from the feet." Muttered the not-so-silent sergeant, unable to bear the tense silence.

"For me, it's the coins on their eyes. Usually it's a fifty-kopek piece each." Added the gravedigger.

"Yeah. That's about one shot of booze for each nose in the air. More noses up – more for us…" Kalenyk waved his hand, as usual.

The group walked on, helpless. Naturally. Because helplessness can't be faked – it has no switch, no toggle.

"And the deceased – God forgive him – didn't leave a trace. Not even, well, urine… no shirt, no sock." Stirred the major's professional conscience. "And you drunks!.." he now snapped at the grave-diggers.

"Only great people have great, let's say, flaws." Said the not-so-silent sergeant, patting Kalenyk's friend on the shoulder.

Leaves fell from the trees like continents. Sleepy and plentiful. Thought flickered around again with no navel-strings attached. You could hear the hum of underground rivers, like poets: they exist, but are not always needed, invisible and real.

They know the language of grass and deer, who can speak – but won't speak to people, killers, cannibals. Iron, meanwhile, doesn't know how to speak at all…

"Good deeds don't go unnoticed. Initiative gets punished." Kalenyk's friend muttered to himself. "We meant well, wanted to resurrect a guy – and ended up with the cops."

"Don't whine! Look what happened – he actually came back. The client resurrected, or what?" said the major.

Young sorrow kissed old joy, and the shadows of birds taking flight floated across waters brighter than themselves like castles.

Everything felt like a guelder rose's dream. Autumn – not death, but sleep.

"You, Kalenyk, with your chronic truth-telling, don't go causing trouble. If you blab about resurrection to some chick – some dumb goose – she'll faint flat on the spot. And stupidity is contagious." The gravedigger muttered half-smiling.

"Oh, but it's bliss to be a little stupid. To believe…" replied Kalenyk.

The drunk fools, slowly, windily, but steadily, were transforming into philosopher-psychologists. But true adequacy of thought to being was still far off.

"I'm not afraid of scars." The silent sergeant suddenly burst out. "What I fear is being hit there again… I'm afraid to step back into my grandfather's empty house. But otherwise, no...not graves, not death, not resurrection…"

Everyone fell silent.

The natural balance remained intact. It would be like if the plump-faced cat Boomba suddenly spoke to its owner – he'd be struck speechless...

* * *

All the men finally made it to the stewardess's house. Music was already playing inside. Simple and profound, something modern in a good way – an arrangement of "When I die, bury me" or something like that.

The Siberians were celebrating the Resurrection.

Roughly. Fur-clad. Broadly.

Kryshtalsky didn't tell any stories of his own – he just answered questions, with irony and vigor.

By the third round, as usual, they'd forgotten whose birthday it was.

Someone fired a shotgun. Someone hugged the gravediggers and the cops.

The drunken clarity of Resurrection pierced every human vulnerability.

Only shiny old cat Boomba lay unbothered on the stove, purring about something. In a pot, Japanese cherry blossoms and Sudanese mallow bloomed snow-pale and tender.

An autumnal Easter-ness of being, its organic orgiastic quality, knew nothing and understood everything – wise in the openness of its admission.

Words really weren't needed, and yet without them, something felt wrong.

The longing violin music pulled somewhere.

The stewardess's old father was taking photos.

Someone posed.

The hunters knew how to pose in front of rifles aimed at them.

But none of them knew how to pose in front of eternity.

* * *

Some were prisoners or lovers of Fate. Others had just been struck by Chance, which, in the end, had changed their Fate. All of them were subject to Space and Time – aging bodies, all the same.

The major suggested they go to the cemetery – to the opened grave – but either no one heard, or it was already too late to organize any kind of procession, and so the wake on the grave never happened.

They cried and laughed. Lied – globally, not specifically.

"You scream loud?" Kalenyk hugged Kryshtalsky.

"You know, there's a parable about that." Kryshtalsky said. "A guy's yelling in the forest – yelling and yelling, until a bear shows up. Says, 'Why are you screaming, man?' And the guy goes, 'I just want someone to hear me.' And the bear says, 'Well, I heard you. Does it make you feel better?'"

Kalenyk nodded bitterly. "Sic transit gloria mundi."

And then the dancing started. Wordless dancing.

"What matters is where you fall – face forward – meaning, where you're heading. Not the fact that you escape a fall." The quiet sergeant said to himself.

CHANCE AND FATE

"That Power I serve which wills forever evil yet does forever good," Fate said to Chance instead of a greeting, quoting herself – she once dictated that very line to old Goethe for his Faust.

He kissed her on the cheek.

"Sorry, I really don't have time today. I've got ballroom dancing at eighteen hundred sharp." She went on. "Don't be surprised. Something came over me. I'm Olesia Sokolovska now. I'm in Singapore. Fantastic opera house there."

"Oh, the opera!" Chance threw up his hands. "And I was going to invite you, Countess Sokolovska... with a name like that."

"Look, old man, let's keep it simple. Aren't there enough of those various spirits in the world already? And you still want to turn me into a woman...with a child, with fruit."

"But it's out of love." Chance replied, lightly and playfully, losing any hint of depth.

"I'm busy right now. I'm really interested in stealing away that resurrected guy – 24-Y-315 – from a certain stewardess. Resurrected, you could say. So I'm pretending to be this girl Sokolovska. Got it?"

Chance had nothing more to say, except to himself:

"Want to start over? It's easy. And it's hard."

Fate heard that too, and also, as if to herself, said:

"I want to grow a diamond, Lord forgive me, with my own hands. I hope Loa won't mind. And He, She, It is asleep anyway.

I want music!.. Music untouched by hands. Or maybe touched?"

FATE AND TARAS KRYSHTALSKYI

"You scared me..."

"How?"

"With your beauty..."

That was the first line of the second accidental meeting between Taras Kryshtalskyi and Olesia Sokolovska. The first – an encounter-introduction – was at a poetry festival where they'd been hanging out.

Now Taras kissed the young lady on the cheek, almost on the lips. In his veins, like a fish in underground rivers, flashed a celestial-intimate yearning. Olesia was beautiful and spiritually elevated, the kind of diamond that makes you forget everything once you've found it.

The mystic magic of her hair, the crane-like gaze of her heart, the smoky grace of her milky-stubborn body...After everything he'd lived through, after returning to the edge of Europe, Taras was almost unafraid of life. The stewardess kept sending him angry, shrill letters, but he no longer replied. Only the strong admit their mistakes, laugh into the void, and do what brings them joy. Old things are as magical as undiscovered lands, but one must still choose.

Taras and Olesia walked through the city, drank juice. They began talking about business to fill the pauses, but autumn danced all around them. And it felt good, as if their bodies lacked souls.

Kryshtalskyi reads both his own and others' poems, and Olesia was fascinated by their musicality. Like children, they boasted about their achievements: Kryshtalskyi's play was being staged at the theater, Sokolovska danced in Swan Lake – they found it both natural and difficult to unite the real with the artistic, what belonged to the Caesar's with what belonged to...

Together, they imagined themselves lying in hay, together, sidestepping insinuations from afar, subconsciously relying on Chance.

And Chance, jealous of his "old flame" Fate, decided to "inhabit" earthly beings so he could be near his Fate, for both Space and Time have Fate. In his place, he left his Computer – just as Fate had done.

Now the Computers of Chance and Fate worked together, joined, while their owners luxuriated on one of the little planets where Loa was cultivating himself – spiritual diamonds that, like natural diamonds, had to be pure, true-parallel (adequate), strong, immortal – and (despite all that) alive, capable of reproduction, of giving birth to similar selves, like Loa.

Pearl farmers had learned to grow pearls (it takes six years for them to mature), and the Creator's farmers – Fate, Time, Chance, Space, Death – were doing the same, in their holy and sinful way.

Kryshtalskyi and Sokolovska were already holding hands – just as cosmic music merges with oceanic, just as the mistake of the sage Columbus is blissful, just as the path matters more than the goal, just as frogs are beautiful and peacocks are impractical...

Fate and Taras mischievously awaited Something and played, played, played with cool, hair-soft balls made of their own breaths, blinking as they drew closer.

The people who were inhabited by Fate and Chance would shudder immediately, sensing some inner shift, but usually blamed it on the weather or their advanced age – meaning they noticed nothing out of the ordinary, brushing it off as a game of chance, fate...a glint in the eye, a quickened heartbeat.

Adventuress-Fate lied to herself that she loved this Game. The key – don't pour too much water on the fire, just drops, sips – they only stir it up, because he has something to struggle against, because he is a Man, an Artist...But is there really a difference between Artist and Creator?

Kryshtalskyi was ready to meet Fate if only because, having deconstructed harmony with algebra, he realized he understood "nothing at all", missed harmony – and gave himself to it, stronger and simpler now.

Paradoxically navel-less, childless gods were becoming believers, not computers; girls were becoming beautiful, not aging. He smiled more often and accepted things as they were, calmly, without the desire for truth, "which we don't need". Almost.

Lady History whispered with sensitively stubborn lips something about the evolution of peoples and their gods – fetishism, animism, spirits, demons. Ashur was the god of the Assyrians,

Yahweh the tribal god of Israel, Marduk the chief god of Babylon.
In Egypt (alternately): Horus, Ptah, Amun, Ra. Deism, Pantheism,
Deism...The gods of conquered peoples were given subordinate
places in the polytheistic pantheon.

Indeed:

...Soul has lowered the bar.
The dead are dying at last
The wheat has grown through the pyramids
And prickles the aliens' feet.
Every morning our Sculptor
Stares in the looking glass
Where God, carved by this world
Is what he is going to meet.

Taras Kryshtalskyi, poem, translated by Matvii Smirnov.

So it is..."A poet isn't a fountain, but a sponge..." Yahweh
was a tribal god, and when the Jewish state was formed (the tribes
united), Yahweh became the Almighty. Transformation...In Christianity, the one God already has three hypostases: the Father, the
Son, and the Holy Spirit.

It's precisely the third hypostasis that constantly needs to
be nourished with spirit-diamonds: SO THAT LOA DOES NOT
FLICKER OUT. Everything else is a matter of faith – without it,
evil can be constructive, and good destructive, and in general –
there is no balance, and thus – no life, which beauty is unlikely
to save, but deceit might...The only question is: where's the limit?

"This."

"That's so funny!" said Olesia Sokolovska. "I sat down near
a church to rest, glanced around – and people started crossing
themselves at me..."

"Hm..."

"I mean, of course they're crossing themselves at the church,
but still, it feels like..."

Taras laughed, thinking to himself: if someone sits down near
a toilet...Deceit, deceit. Either deceive yourself, or deceive others.
Metaphor, image. Curiosity. Studying the language of whales, of
flowers rustling in the eyes of cranes, the silence of stars waiting
for us, probably, because "eternal peace will hardly delight the heart,

eternal peace is the destiny of pyramids, but for a falling star, there is only a moment, a dazzling moment."

"We are threads in the web, but we are not the ones who weave it." Said a Native chief – Taras carried Olesia over a stream.

"Well, whether we are or aren't – that's still unknown." Fate smiled enigmatically through Olesia's lips.

Taras felt like he was on cloud nine. He was beside himself. Of course – because now, instead of a guardian angel, he was accompanied by Chance itself, whose aura was powerful but not oppressive. Kryshtalskyi, of course, didn't know, but he felt it. Like a birdlike Martian language, he studied his own soul, especially fascinating during its cracks and ascents, Christian sins that existed everywhere – like the dusk and dawn of the star we call the Sun.

Fate and Chance wandered on, philosophizing and psychologizing through the mouths of Olesia Sokolovska and Taras Kryshtalskyi, who eventually agreed that Kryshtalskyi would speak to the director, and in his play, *Divination on the Ages*, the role of Fate would be played by her – Sokolovska.

They met again and again, spent time in salons and in forests, drank wine and milk, but never came any closer to each other than a kiss at the corner of the lips.

Time and Space looked after them like caring parents, smiling knowingly.

They attended the rehearsals. Kryshtalskyi got himself a diamond ring for the pinky of his left hand and gave Olesia a pair of diamond earrings.

They quarreled with the director, gave suggestions, searched for money for costumes, because "divining on the ages" wasn't so easy, even for the folk sorcerers – so it was said among the people.

And they had worthy enemies.

The premiere of Divination on the Ages was to be held on January 13, 2000, at the twilight of time, the gap between the old and the new calendar styles.

Odyssey...Diamandea...Iliad. It had to be like a nativity play, where gods of various tribes and nations wear masks – where Death, Fate, Chance, Space, and Time appear...where the Creator-Wind breathes, where grasses, ants, and stars converse with one another.

Where all is one, and each one is Person, Creator.

Hey!

Watch for the posters.

The performance must be free – by Faustian-Mephistophelian passes.

The most important thing is to find a soulful sponsor.

Amen.

Footnotes:

Page 1. Leningrad: The name of Russian city of Saint-Petersburg through Soviet period. Perceived by Russian as a centre of culture and art.

Page 43. Banderite: A follower of Stepan Bandera's armed movement for Ukraine's independence from Soviets and Germans in the first half of the 20th century

Page 60. Nativity Fast: In Eastern Christianity, a 40-day period of fasting before Christmas

Page 71. Kurgan Stelae: Kurgan stelae are ancient stone anthropomorphic monuments found across the steppe regions of Ukraine, typically set near or on kurgans (burial mounds). Dating from the Bronze Age through the medieval period, they are associated with steppe cultures such as the Scythians and later Turkic nomads, and are thought to have served ritual, commemorative, or ancestral functions.

Page 77. Polissian: Native to Polissia, a historical region of north-western Ukraine

III

COSSACK MAMAY DANCE

Poems by
Ihor Pavlyuk

Translated by
Matvii Smirnov

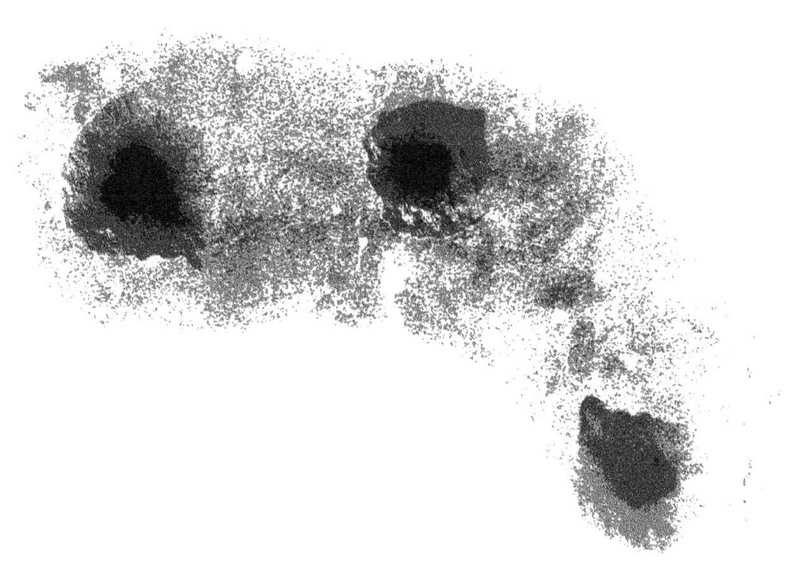

THE BLIND

A no-man's land. A place of fiends and angels
Where light and life come at a dear price.
Here in the dark a blind man is your ranger
He hears the creak of gates of paradise.

He can mistake a cuddle for a snare
He trips and falls and rises up again.
In these mysterious ways he gives his care
He heals the buds of wounds and cures the pain.

The blind man is a poet. He caresses
The cosmic waves, the human hearts. He knows
The secret of the maiden's trembling tresses
That hide your heart away from greedy crows.

His naked skin can feel a strong sensation
Of lights in human souls, but also filth.
His faith does not require explanation
He loves the things the world destroys and kills.

He thinks of heaven every waking hour,
The devil's claws that scratch so hard and deep.
He sees the ghouls with their unholy power,
Those you avoid of meeting in your sleep.

Let people gossip, let them talk and swear–
Those slaves of hell,oh let them moan and hiss,
I will continue whispering my prayer
And talk to God about my pain and bliss,

That's all there is. The rest is but illusion–
All that I lose, and everything I gain.
I seek amidst the darkness and confusion
No, not the earthly light – the holy grain.

A MEETING WITH AN OLD VETERAN FRIEND

I met my friend from the good old days
For a pint of stout.
We had our sorrows to drink away,
We talked about

Our friends at sea – some still alive,
Some travelled far,
About our times that rumbled like
A railway car,

We drank to all those dated things
What were they, though?
The sins and worries that in spring
Would melt like snow?

The dream of Lenin's paradise
Had gone away.
No need to rush – the one who dies
Shall have his wake.

So, there we were, the beer was cold,
Young was the night,
It felt so early, the trees were gold,
It felt so nice,

The chirping swallows swung in haste
And flew across.
I heard the medals clink against
His iron cross,

And then I gave him the book I wrote.
So, there we sat –
Two sober men by the endless road,
So clear, so sad.

FROM THE CYCLE "SPRING AND WAR"

This pointless war has scarred my soul and mind
These words are weak, incapable of telling
The truth. I've lost my faith in humankind
I'm frightened like an orphan under shelling.

I've lost my guiding star, I've lost myself,
My blood went mute and I can't hear its call.
The master sent to war his voiceless serf –
Like many times before, he'll fight and fall.

This cosmic grief; this butchery on Earth
It is not done to us for home or pride,
This spring of mine is stained with war and death,
And all our faith in humankind has died.

The fighter jets instead of birds above
Are silver crucifixes in the sky…
We humans lost humanity and love –
God and the Devil know the reason why.

A MONOLOGUE OF THE CROSS-LIKE

Crosses stand on the crossways.
Mist and sorrow prevail.
Fire, stars and the sun rays,
Temples, taverns and jail.

Waves of light, warm and gentle
Girls on brooms in the sky
Tender kiss of a candle.
Flocks of cranes flying by
My old soul, tired, wrinkled,
Stir my blood, cold and still

I will chase my horilka
With the Dnipro's large swill

I'll lie down and sleep here
On these clouds, soft and blue.

By a thousand years
I am older than you.

IMMORTALITY OF WATER

Water's dying...
We're searching for glory, we're marching
Through the minefields of fate, so determined and yet terrified
Placing goblets of brew on the linen of snow, crisp and starchy,
Riverbeds under ice we are seeking and struggling to find.

Water – iced, vapourised...
Even fog's merely sunbeams and water.
In this world, water gets resurrected when temperature's low
And Your body that shines like a tear growing hotter and hotter
Legless sorrow can shatter your wings as a floating ice floe.

Water drips on a rock...
Turning red like this dusk that is falling
For the evening twilight is more beautiful than the day's dawn,
Deathly scaffolds can turn into pedestals, splendid and solemn
And "the soft beats the hard", as they say, every time, on and on.

All shall pass in the end. Only water and light will be there
To remind us of hearts that once sang and rejoiced, but alas
Cosmic darkness and chaos are black as a pelt of a bear
Water dies, water lives, resurrected again. Human–glass...

NOWADAYS

Having washed myself in snow
I am just a little hare.
Hordes surrounding Kyiv grow,
Drones are rattling in the air.

Brothers dead, and son's at war.
I will douse the global fire
Glory, cash, and chicks, and more…
I've said no to all desires.

Giving blood, donating, praying
I direct the humankind
To the stars. Like cards, I'm playing
With tectonic plates of mind.

Through the dense and thorny forest
I advanced, I swam and flew
Trees were standing like a chorus
Words were hollow as a flute.

All entwined – outside, inside us:
Lightning flashes, cold as ice,
Golden threads of anxious sirens,
Roads that lead to paradise.

Snow is falling.
Earth's like heaven.
Frozen joy.
A witch.
A cat.
Snow-white swan
(black as a raven) –
Promise of a tit-for-tat.

TO MY BROTHER

My brother – remember the time we had?
Neither of us was a saint.
Here is my water and here is my bread
But I will not shake your hand.
Here is my water and here is my bread…

I feel searing pain right between my wings
From the wound that your knife has made.
You may get the justice that God will bring
Unless He too is betrayed.

My brother, we went together through war
And crosses like bulwarks were tall.
But you sold your soul to them like a whore –
Did it help you at all?

So, are you rich? Did you make enough
At least for a glass of kvass –
From your betrayal, from selling us?
You've done this before, alas.

You've shown no mercy, but still at a loss?
Come here, I'll give you the rest.
The line we've crossed should not have been crossed –
Here on Earth we're guests.

We were no saints, you and I, as we went
Through the troubles that lied ahead.
And even though I have lost my hand
I'll hand you my water and bread
Here is my water and bread

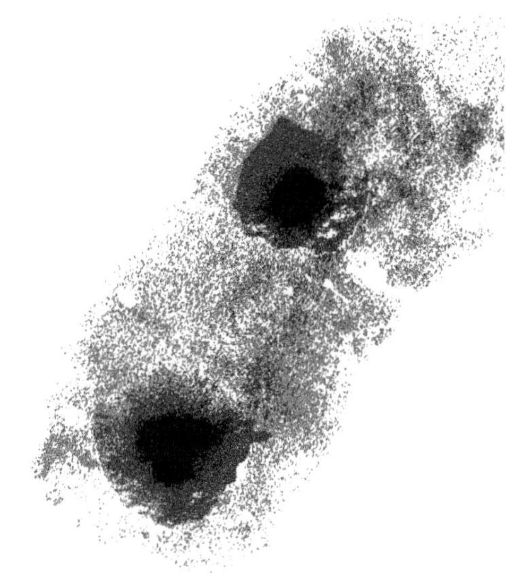

BIOGRAPHY

Ihor Pavlyuk is a Ukrainian writer, translator and research worker. He is a Doctor of Social Communication, professor. He is a recipient of the 2013 English PEN Award, Winner of the Switzerland Literary Prize 2021 and is a member of the English PEN and the European Society of Authors. He has participated in various international literary festivals, including Estonia, Georgia, Russia, Belarus, Germany, Italy, the United States of America, Poland, Turkey, Ireland, Pakistan, England, Czech Republic and international editions about Ukrainians from Volyn region, Ukrainian writers and poets.

Currently, Pavlyuk is leading researcher of Taras Shevchenko Institute of Literature of the National Academy of Sciences of Ukraine in Kiev, professor of Ukrainian media, Ivan Franko National University of Lviv.

Works of Ihor Pavlyuk have been translated into Russian, Belarusian, Polish, English, French, Latvian, Bulgarian, Japanese and other languages and published in such magazines as *The Apple Valley Review*, Volume 7, Number 2 (Fall 2012), *Muddy River Poetry Review*, Asymptote, *Gold Dust* (Issue 23), *The Adirondack Review*, *The Recusant, Metamorphoses, Eurasia Review*, *The World Poets Quarterly*, and many others.

Ihor Pavlyuk is the protagonist of the film *Between Bug and God* and the film *Voice*. American and British actors read poems by Ihor Pavlyuk. Books of Ihor Pavlyuk's lyric poetry appeared at the crossroads behind the cordon: USA (2011), Russia (2012), Poland (2012), England (2013), France (2015), USA (2019, 2020). His book *A Flight over the Black Sea* became the winning book within Writers in Translation competition by English PEN club.

* * *

https://en.wikipedia.org/wiki/Ihor_Pavlyuk
https://uk.wikipedia.org/wiki/Павлюк_Ігор_Зиновійович